SPORTS SCANDALS

TRUE STORIES OF CHEATING, CORRUPTION AND GREED

NORMAN FERGUSON

summersdale

6445978

SPORTS SCANDALS

SPORTS SCANDALS

Summersdale Publishers Ltd
46 West Street
Chichester
West Sussex
PO19 1RP
UK

www.summersdale.com

Printed and bound by CPI Group (UK) Ltd, Croydon, CR0 4YY

ISBN: 978-1-84953-911-1

Substantial discounts on bulk quantities of Summersdale books are available to corporations, professional associations and other organisations. For details contact Nicky Douglas by telephone: +44 (0) 1243 756902, fax: +44 (0) 1243 786300 or email: nicky@summersdale.com.

Disclaimer: Every effort has been made to ensure that the information in this book was correct at the time of publication. If errors or developments relating to the cases herein are brought to the attention of the author and publisher, they would be happy to make amendments in any future reprints or new editions of the work.

CONTENTS

INTRODUCTION

No one who watched the men's 100m final at the 1988 Olympics in Seoul will ever forget how Canada's Ben Johnson powered down the track like his victory was never in doubt. He crossed the line in world-record time with his index finger raised to confirm his status: number one. It could easily have represented 'number one cheater' as within days he was on his way home, stripped of his medal and world record, his career in tatters in a blaze of global publicity over his use of performance-enhancing drugs.

The motives behind cheating, corruption and general naughtiness in sport are not all that different from those found in politics, business or even everyday life. Wherever there are people, you will find a certain amount of greed, lust, ambition and insecurity. But sports stars are held up to us as role models, and the extraordinary pressure on them to conduct themselves accordingly means that, when it happens, their fall from grace is all the greater (and better reported).

In the following pages I've brought together some of the best known of these scandals, stretching back more than a hundred years, from ungentlemanly Victorian cricketers to modern-day philandering footballers. And you'll also find some less well known but still rather remarkable true stories. The chapters are themed according to the type of scandal rather than the sport, and each one begins with a 'key scandal' which is arguably the juiciest or most famous example. Apart from that, the entries in each chapter are in chronological order, from earliest to most recent, but some miscreants have scandalised us across multiple years, so sometimes their mischief is gathered together in one place for your reading pleasure.

BAD BEHAVIOUR: SEX

Sportsmen and women work hard to prepare their bodies for competition, spending hours at the gym or training ground. Once their events are over they are just as susceptible as anyone else to the illicit pleasures of the flesh. With their levels of fame hardly acting as a deterrent to dalliances, the sporting sex scandal has been a familiar feature in the media for years.

KEY SCANDAL: TIGER IN THE ROUGH

Achievements on the golf course are only part of setting an example. Character and decency are what really count. Parents used to point to me as a role model for their kids. I owe all of those families a special apology. I want to say to them that I am truly sorry.

Tiger Woods, 19 February 2010

Just what had led to the most accomplished, successful and famous golfer of the modern era having to apologise in such an uncomfortable and public way?

Tiger Woods had burst on to the sporting stage in 1997 when he won his first major tournament at the US Masters in

Augusta, Georgia, by 12 strokes, shooting a score of 18 under par. Both were records that still stand. Being just 21 at the time, he created another record by being the youngest ever winner.

His prodigious talent saw him go on to win a further 13 major tournaments and he looked certain to overhaul the record of 18, held by golfing legend Jack Nicklaus.

With the success on the fairway and greens came lucrative sponsorships deals. Companies paid well to have this gentle-speaking giant of the game on board. Nike signed Woods in 1996 for $40 million over five years. This amount was doubled for his next contract with them in 2001.

Professional triumphs mirrored personal fulfilment off the golf course: Woods was married in 2004 to the Swedish-American model and au pair Elin Nordegren. The couple had two children, born in 2007 and 2009.

On the night of 27 November 2009 police were called to the Woods residence in Windermere, near Orlando, Florida. In what was called 'the car crash heard round the world', Woods' Cadillac Escalade SUV had been driven into a tree, 150 feet from his home at 2.30 a.m. On the way, the SUV had been driven into a hedge and a fire hydrant. Woods was found lapsing into unconsciousness at the scene and taken to hospital. At first it was suggested that his wife had smashed the rear windows of the SUV to help get him out of the crashed vehicle, but it was later revealed that she had smashed the rear window with a golf club in a rage as Woods fled his house following an argument.

Woods was cited for a small traffic violation for careless driving, but the matter wasn't about to end there. Two days before the crash a US tabloid had printed a story about an affair Woods was alleged to have had with a nightclub hostess in New York. This was only the beginning. Soon one of the biggest media storms involving a sportsperson erupted as more and more allegations began to emerge about infidelities by the world's number-one golfer.

In December 2009, Woods announced a break from professional golf to concentrate on his family. He was divorced in August 2010.

After the scandal, companies backed away and firms such as AT&T and General Motors tore up their sponsorship deals, but while Woods' form on the golf course never revived to his previous levels he was still very bankable. *Golf Digest* magazine reported he made $55 million in 2014 – 99 per cent of this came via endorsements.

MRS BROWN'S BOY

While football players are more commonly reported on for their off-the-pitch activities, it is not unknown for managers and coaching staff to appear in the media. This scandal in particular involved one of England's most famous clubs.

Tommy Docherty was a Scottish manager renowned for his ready quips, but this overshadowed his talent as a manager. After being in charge of Chelsea, Queens Park Rangers, Aston Villa, Porto and Scotland's national team, he joined Manchester United in 1972. Docherty became the first manager to see Manchester United relegated, but the attacking style of football his team produced saw them bounce straight back.

In May 1977 the Old Trafford side won the FA Cup, their first victory of the famous trophy for 14 years. But the manager didn't have long to enjoy his success, as it was revealed soon after that Docherty, who was married, was having an affair with Mary Brown, who was also married – to the club's physiotherapist.

Docherty was sacked for breaching his contract, but his relationship with Mary Brown resulted in a long-lasting marriage. In 2013 he said: 'When I got the sack from Manchester United after my affair it didn't matter. She's worth twenty Manchester Uniteds.'

SEX, LINES AND VIDEOTAPE

In 1998 two footballers made a sex tape that no one else would have seen had one of the participants destroyed it, rather than throwing it in the rubbish where a reporter discovered it. The rubbish rubbish-thrower-outer was Manchester United forward Dwight Yorke and his partner in crime was Australian goalkeeper Mark Bosnich who was playing for Aston Villa at the time.

The players had set up a hidden camera to record their exploits with four women, and the video showed them dressing up in women's clothes and Bosnich being spanked.

Bosnich was no stranger to bad headlines. In October 1996 he had been in trouble for giving a Nazi salute while playing for Aston Villa against Tottenham Hotspur. In a game the year before, Bosnich had knocked Spurs' German forward Jürgen Klinsmann unconscious with his knee. When Spurs fans started chanting 'Klinsmann!' at Bosnich, he reacted by giving the salute, and at the same time putting his index finger across his top lip, to imitate Hitler's moustache. Spurs has a strong Jewish following. The Australian claimed he was imitating John Cleese's character Basil Fawlty but apologised, saying, 'If it had been intentional, I should be in jail.' He was fined £1,000 by the Football Association (FA).

In June 1999, a day after signing for Manchester United, Bosnich was arrested on his stag night for allegedly grabbing a photographer's camera outside a lap-dancing club. He was released just in time to make it to the hotel for his big day.

Bosnich joined Chelsea after leaving Manchester United in 2001 but was sacked when he was found to have taken cocaine. His habit saw him enter a clinic for treatment. He returned to Australia and played several games before finally retiring in 2009, when he became a television pundit.

HUMPED

It was a bitter humiliation for Israel's national football team when they were beaten 8–0 on aggregate by Denmark in a play-off for Euro 2000. But when it was revealed that some players had spent the night before the first leg with prostitutes, it turned into a full-blown scandal. The Israeli Internal Security Minister at the time, Shlomo Ben-Ami, tried to keep a sense of humour when he said, 'If it had been the Danish players who partied with call girls, the result would have been the same.'

SCORING FOR FUN

Now retired, Ally McCoist was a footballing Scot with a quick wit – almost as quick as his eye for a goal. When talking about the English rugby team Wasps, he wondered if they had a B Team.

McCoist began his career at St Johnstone in Scotland, then played in England at Sunderland before joining Rangers in

1983, where he became a firm favourite of the fans – if not of managers such as Graeme Souness. 'Super Ally' once got into trouble with the renowned hard man Souness for going to Cheltenham to see the horse racing rather than resting on an official day off. Despite his manager's displeasure, McCoist's career at the Glasgow club didn't come to an end and he went on to score a total of 355 goals for Rangers, a club record.

As he neared the end of his playing career, McCoist found success on TV as a football pundit and also as a team captain on the BBC panel show *A Question of Sport*.

In 2001 he found himself in another type of trouble when his affair with actress and singer Patsy Kensit became public. Not only that, but it was revealed he was also having an affair with an air stewardess. In a scenario that would not have been out of place in TV drama *Footballers' Wives*, it turned out that while McCoist was trying to reconcile with his wife Allison, she had been seeing their landscape gardener. The couple divorced in 2004.

ROONEY!

Scouse footballer Wayne Rooney will be remembered for many things: being the youngest player to represent England (at the time), being England's youngest ever scorer, England's highest scorer (51 goals by the end of 2015) and being the winner of numerous titles and cups for his club side Manchester United.

Unfortunately, the Liverpudlian will also be remembered for frequenting prostitutes.

In 2004 Rooney admitted visiting massage parlours and prostitutes when younger, something he apologised for, saying,

'I now regret it deeply and hope people may understand it was the sort of mistake you make when you are young and stupid.' One of the prostitutes he frequented was a grandmother.

In 2010 the *Sunday Mirror* reported that Rooney paid for sex sessions with a prostitute seven times over a four-month period. It was claimed that he was seeing Jennifer Thompson while his wife Coleen Rooney was pregnant with their first child, and that Thompson charged £1,000 a night, a marked difference from the £45 that Rooney was said to have paid when he was younger.

SWEET FA

Sven-Göran Eriksson was a quiet, bespectacled figure who looked more like a kindly physics teacher than a man tasked with marshalling the high-powered egos of professional football players. But this image belied a shrewd manager who had been in charge of teams in countries such as Italy, Portugal and his home nation of Sweden. In 2001 he became manager of England – the first foreign national to be in charge of the team.

In August 2004, the *News of the World* revealed that Eriksson had been having an affair with Faria Alam, the PA of David Davies, executive director of the Football Association. The tabloid divulged that Alam had also had a relationship with Mark Palios, the FA's chief executive. At the time, Eriksson had a partner, the Italian lawyer Nancy Dell'Olio.

While the initial story was a traditional sex scandal, it quickly became a bigger affair relating to how the FA had handled the situation. It became clear that they had wished to focus the attention on Eriksson rather than their chief executive. The *News of the World* printed the transcript of a taped conversation in which the FA's director of communications, Colin Gibson, discussed adopting this strategy. He suggested he could offer up details on Eriksson's private life if Palios were left out of future stories. Alam was quoted in the *News of the World* saying, 'The scandal was not his [Eriksson's] affair with me; the scandal is how the FA set about covering it up.'

Palios and Gibson resigned as a result of the furore and Alam later moved to Canada. Eriksson remained England manager until 2006.

RONALDON'T

Brazilian star forward Ronaldo had been selected for his nation's World Cup-winning team in 1994 at the age of just 17. Although he didn't play, he would go on to glory by scoring the two winning goals in the final of the 2002 World Cup, where he also picked up the Golden Boot award for scoring the most goals in the tournament. After losing form, in April 2008 he was home in Rio de Janeiro, recovering from knee surgery.

One night, after dropping off his girlfriend, he decided his evening's entertainment was not over and picked up three prostitutes – but when he discovered they were in fact transvestites, he kicked off. The world-famous footballer was reported to have tried to buy their silence and two of the prostitutes each took R$1,000 (£300), while the other attempted to extort R$50,000 (£15,000) from him.

The three-time FIFA World Player of the Year denied allegations that he tried to buy drugs and that he threatened to hit one of the prostitutes. Police were called and after their investigation Rio's police superintendent Carlos Augusto Nogueira commented, 'Ronaldo said he just wanted to amuse himself – that's not a crime.' The star admitted it was 'the stupidest mistake of my life'.

TERRY'S NOT ALL GOLD

In 2010 tabloid newspapers printed allegations that Chelsea and England captain John Terry had been having a sexual relationship with a former teammate's ex-girlfriend. Terry had attempted to obtain a superinjunction to keep his private life private, but his plans were foiled.

Terry, who was known for his commanding leadership on the pitch, saw his reputation damaged for an alleged affair with Vanessa Perroncel, the ex-girlfriend of Wayne Bridge, who had played at Stamford Bridge alongside Terry until January 2009. Terry had been married since 2007. He lost the England captaincy as a result of the scandal. Perroncel's denials of any physical affair were ignored as story after story went into detail.

Bridge retired from international football, saying, 'I believe my position in the squad is now untenable and potentially divisive. I feel for the sake of the team and in order to avoid what will be inevitable distractions, I have decided not to put myself forward for selection.'

Terry was no stranger to public controversies. In 2001 he was fined by his club after he and some teammates drunkenly mocked American tourists following the 11 September terrorist attacks, and the following year he missed being called up to the England squad for the 2002 World Cup as he was awaiting trial for the assault of a doorman, for which he was acquitted.

In 2009 he was reportedly available to give guided tours of Stamford Bridge for cash and he was criticised for having a marketing company tout his availability for endorsements before the 2010 World Cup. The following year, he was embroiled in a racism row following on-field comments made to Queens Park Rangers player Anton Ferdinand, for which he was fined £220,000 and banned for four matches.

KEEPING IT IN THE FAMILY

Welsh international winger Ryan Giggs played for only one league club during his professional career: Manchester United. Unfortunately, he wasn't as loyal in his private life, when in May 2011 it was revealed he'd been having an affair with his brother's wife.

Giggs had met Natasha Lever, his future sister-in-law, in early 2003 before she began going out with his brother Rhodri. Rhodri and Natasha married in June 2010, a few months before Giggs started a six-month affair with another woman: Imogen Thomas, a former Miss Wales and contestant on TV reality show *Big Brother*.

The revelations about Giggs' affair emerged after Thomas spoke publicly about her relationship with a professional footballer. Married since 2007, Giggs had tried to suppress the Imogen Thomas story with a £150,000 superinjunction, but it leaked through social media and the *Sunday Herald* newspaper printed on its front cover a thinly disguised image of his face.

Natasha then went public about their eight-year affair, which had ended in April 2011. She was upset at being two-timed by Giggs. Rhodri found out about the affair when his mother brought round the newspapers on the morning the story broke.

In 2012 Natasha's time in the spotlight had been enough to earn her a place on *Celebrity Big Brother*. The following year Natasha and Rhodri divorced.

The Giggs brothers didn't speak for years after the affair was made public, but in 2015 they were seen together, apparently attempting to reconcile their relationship.

Their aunt Joanna Wilson said of Ryan in 2011: 'One thing's for sure – he can't keep his trousers up and he needs help for it.'

LOVE MATCH

In 1985 Boris Becker burst on to the scene as a dynamic 17-year-old tennis player when he won Wimbledon. He went on to win six major tournaments in total, but in 1999 the German found his way into the media glare with a performance that led to an appearance in a different kind of court.

After exiting Wimbledon at the racquet of Pat Rafter, Becker was in London's trendy Nobu restaurant when one thing led to another and he had sex with a Russian model called Angela Ermakova, who was working as a waitress. This quickly completed act of lovemaking was said to have taken place in a broom cupboard. Becker went on his way and thought no more about it until eight months later he received news that he was going to be a father. He denied it initially, but DNA tests proved otherwise. Ermakova had a girl, named Anna.

Not long after, Becker's wife Barbara, with whom he had two children, divorced him. He married for the second time in 2009, to Lilly Kerssenberg, and had a child with her as well.

Having retired from playing tennis in 1999, he became a coach to world number one Novak Djokovic, and his Teutonic tones are often heard on TV commentary.

BAD BEHAVIOUR: ALCOHOL

In facing such high expectations from their fans, it's not surprising that sportsmen and women sometimes look for escapism in an alcoholic beverage or two. Or too many. And as they are public figures, their misdemeanours caused by the demon drink receive greater attention than the man or woman (lying down drunk) in the street.

KEY SCANDAL: CALCUTTA CUP KICKED

The international rugby match played between Scotland and England each year forms part of the Six Nations Championship. The fixture also decides the winner of the Calcutta Cup, which has been awarded since 1879. The trophy was devised by the Calcutta Football Club when they were wound up in 1877. They withdrew all their club funds and had the silver rupees melted down and made into the 18-inch trophy. The ornate design features handles in the shape of cobras.

One of the Calcutta Cup matches that drew extra attention was in 1988, with a closely fought match seeing England winning 9–6. Afterwards, as was the tradition, the players jointly celebrated. The English players were late to the

21

reception and found that the Scots had drunk all the whisky. The home team had started the evening's festivities by drinking a Rusty Nail – a cocktail of Drambuie liqueur and whisky – on the bus back from Murrayfield Stadium.

As the drink flowed, the revelry increased and two fights kicked off between the rival teams. Then there was a food fight, and the teams' officials were pelted with starters, main courses and desserts.

As England had won, they got to choose what alcoholic beverage went into the cup to be passed around. Champagne was duly used and the cup went around the boisterous room. Just as English hooker Brian Moore was about to take a drink, the contents were tipped over his head by Scots player John Jeffrey and England's Dean Richards, who in his day job was a policeman.

Upset, Moore gave chase and Jeffrey and Richards ran out of the hotel and got into a taxi, which took them on a mini pub crawl. One thing led to another and soon there was a mini game of rugby being played down Edinburgh's famous bar-filled boulevard Rose Street. The details are vague, whether through selective memory or the effects of the alcohol, but it appears the beautifully decorated silver trophy was used as a rugby ball and was frequently dropped. And possibly kicked. The condition of the now dented trophy led to the Scottish *Sunday Mail* christening it 'The Calcutta Plate'.

The next morning, as the hangovers took over, thoughts turned to the fact that this might cause a *stushie* – a Scottish word for a scandal or outrage. It did. Jeffrey later said, 'We took it away and it was not damaged and it came back damaged, so you have to hold your hands up and say yes, we were responsible.'

For their part in the incident Jeffrey received a six-month ban and Richards was banned for one match. The Calcutta Cup was repaired and has remained intact so far.

NEVER MIND THE ROWLOCKS

Celtic player Jimmy Johnstone was of the breed of wingers once common in Scottish football. Nicknamed 'Jinky', he had a contemporary at Rangers in Willie Henderson and was later followed by the likes of Davie Cooper, John Robertson and Pat Nevin.

These tricky players had such close control skills that their teammates would give them the ball in order to have a break themselves. Their ability to create chances with accurate crosses, and lend a hand in goal scoring, made them key components of successful teams, and Johnstone was part of the one of the most successful sides.

With Johnstone in the side, Celtic were Britain's first winners of the European Cup in 1967. Playing on the wing with skill and a large measure of cheek meant he was constantly the subject of heavy tackles by opposing defenders, but it was a different challenging environment that was to see Johnstone making headlines in 1974.

Johnstone was part of the Scotland squad for the Home Internationals, which were held annually until 1984. After beating Wales 2–0 at Hampden Park some of the players were allowed out to have a few drinks away from their hotel at Largs, on the Ayrshire coast. Their next game was four days away, the 'big one' against the Auld Enemy: England.

Scotland could win the championships, a perfect send-off to the imminent World Cup in West Germany, where Scotland would be the sole British Isles representative.

While returning to the hotel and passing some rowing boats, Johnstone thought it a good idea to get in one. Teammate Sandy Jardine thought it another good idea to give it gentle push. The boat, with its only passenger on board singing away, drifted out to sea. The boat had no rowlocks for the oars and with no means of navigational control – and not able to swim for shore – Johnstone was at the mercy of the tides. Luckily someone had the foresight to telephone the emergency services and the Scotland star was soon rescued by the coastguard. When he returned to the hotel Johnstone asked what all the fuss was about, saying, 'I thought I'd go fishing.'

There was outrage in the press, but despite the bad headlines Johnstone was picked for the England game and played an important part in the 2–0 win. He went to the World Cup but didn't make an appearance on the pitch. It was thought that his boating escapade plus a pre-tournament drinking session in Oslo with captain Billy Bremner had harmed his chances of gracing football's premier event. Johnstone died in 2006.

TONY ADAMS' DOUBLES

Captain of Arsenal Football Club, Tony Adams was known for being a solid centre-half and for his marshalling of the famous Gunners' defence. In May 1990 his reputation, as well as his car, was to suffer a dent when he crashed his Ford Sierra into a wall while being four times over the legal drink-driving limit. He was found guilty and served 58 days of a four-month sentence in Chelmsford Prison. On his release he returned to his club and led his side to victory twice in the league-and-cup double.

Six years after his conviction, Adams admitted he had a drinking problem. He received support and continued playing before retiring in 2002, having played 669 times for Arsenal and 66 times for England. He then set up a charity called Sporting Chance Clinic to aid sportsmen and women suffering from addiction.

TUILAGI LAGER LAGER

When a team's management are deciding whether or not to allow their players a night out during a major tournament away from home, several factors have to be considered. If they ban nights out they could have on their hands a group of disgruntled players cooped up in a hotel. However, if they let them out and things get out of hand they run the risk of courting bad publicity. The latter happened to England in 2011 at the Rugby World Cup in New Zealand.

England had beaten Argentina in their first game and manager Martin Johnson allowed his players a chance to let off some steam, so they went out in Queenstown. A bar they visited was holding a 'Mad Midget Weekender', although allegations that the team indulged in dwarf-tossing were denied by the players and the bar's manager.

Later the same evening Mike Tindall, England's captain, was filmed via CCTV speaking to a woman who wasn't his wife. (Seven weeks previously he had married the Queen's granddaughter Zara Phillips, daughter of Princess Anne.) The footage was leaked to the press and caused a rumpus.

While this wasn't particularly terrible, Tindall had made matters worse by changing his initial version of events. First he claimed he'd returned to the team's hotel on his own, but had actually gone to another bar with the woman, Jessica Palmer. Matters weren't improved for the England captain when it was revealed that he had once been in a relationship with her. Tindall apologised and was later fined £25,000 and thrown out of the England team's Elite Player Squad, although this fine was later reduced to £15,000 and he was reinstated to the squad on appeal.

This wasn't the end of England's travails. Following their exit from the tournament, there was further trouble when centre Manu Tuilagi jumped from a ferry about to dock in Auckland and swam to the quayside in his underwear. He was fined £3,000 and given a warning by the police. Martin Johnson stated the obvious: 'This was an irresponsible thing to do.'

The competition generated further publicity that the team could have done without:

- The team were issued with a warning after the players' shirt numbers started peeling off their shirts in the game against Argentina, thus making it more difficult for the match referee to identify them. A local printing company was blamed for the mishap. The strips themselves had been criticised as England chose an all-black design for their away kit, mimicking that of the host's famous jerseys.

- Martin Johnson was criticised for allowing players to go bungee jumping and white-water rafting on their days off.

- Players James Haskell and Chris Ashton were both given suspended fines of £5,000 by the Rugby Football Union for making lewd comments to a hotel staff member.

- Underwear-swimmer Manu Tuilagi was fined £5,000 for wearing an unauthorised mouthguard bearing a sponsor's name.

- Following England's game with Romania, two coaches were issued with bans after they changed the ball for two conversions to be taken by Jonny Wilkinson, without permission from the referee. The rules state that the same ball used to score the try should be used for the resultant conversion. The coaches replaced the try ball with one that was felt to be better for kicking. Kicking coach Dave Alred and fitness coach Paul Stridgeon were suspended by England's RFU for the game against Scotland.

URINE TROUBLE

In regards to images of inappropriate behaviour from yesterday, we have cancelled their booking for today.

Tweet from @CheltenhamRaces, 16 March 2016

Horse racing is a chance for punters to get a close look at the sport as racehorses thunder past. Racegoers can also place their bets while having a drink or two. In March 2016, at the Cheltenham Festival, those punters also saw footballers urinating into glasses.

MK Dons player Samir Carruthers and Northampton Town's James Collins were drinking with other footballers in a VIP area at the racecourse. They were photographed urinating into pint glasses. Collins then tipped his over the balcony.

Both players were fined two weeks' wages and both apologised the next day. Carruthers, who had been on the books of Aston Villa and Arsenal, said: 'I just want to say I'm sorry to everyone, my family, the club, chairman, the gaffer.'

Collins, who was on loan from Shrewsbury Town, said: 'I have completely let myself, my family, the fans, and the two clubs that I represent down, and I am sorry to everyone involved.'

MATCH-FIXING

Certain sports lend themselves to being 'fixed', i.e. having their outcome, or parts of their activity, altered for a result favourable to gamblers in the know. Some of sport's biggest scandals have occurred when the offer of money is dangled in front of the participants.

KEY SCANDAL: TENNIS RACKET

If you were to invent a sport that was tailor made for match-fixing the sport that you would invent would be called tennis.

Richard Ings, former head of the ATP Anti-Doping Programme

In January 2016 allegations were made that professional tennis players who had been suspected of match-fixing had escaped proper investigation and punishment. A joint investigation by the BBC and BuzzFeed claimed that investigations by the men's tennis governing authority, the Association of Tennis Professionals (ATP), had highlighted suspicious games in tournaments such as Wimbledon and the French Open, but no player has been subsequently found guilty.

In August 2007 at a tennis tournament being held in Sopot in Poland, the Russian world number four Nikolay

Davydenko was playing the lower-ranked Argentinian player Martín Vassallo Argüello. Davydenko went ahead, as would be expected according to their relative rankings, but the online betting company Betfair noticed that more money than would be expected for such a game was being bet on the outcome. All of it went on Argüello to win. Even more suspect, all this money was coming from a small area of Russia.

When Davydenko went one set up the money continued to be bet against him. Then in the second set, while still ahead, the Russian pulled up injured, so forfeiting the game. Suspecting foul play, Betfair refused to pay out and instead refunded the initial stakes – the first time they had ever done so. As a result, Betfair stopped taking bets on matches featuring certain players. The ATP ordered an inquiry and the players were cleared of any wrongdoing.

Investigations by the BBC and BuzzFeed identified 16 players who repeatedly featured in suspicious matches. Winners of singles and doubles titles at Grand Slam tournaments were among those suspected. The allegations that the ATP had not pursued those players were revealed just before the 2016 Australian Open tournament began. Eight of those players thought to have fixed matches were included in the draw.

After the story broke, a South African player who wished to remain anonymous told the BBC, 'This is like a secret on the tour that everybody knows, but we don't talk about it.'

RUNNING INTO TROUBLE

The 1844 Epsom Derby was won by a horse called Running Rein. Soon after the race was over, protests were raised that the horse wasn't quite what it was said to be.

The previous year, Running Rein had won a race at Newmarket for two year olds and Lord Bentinck, a senior member of the Jockey Club, raised objections, doubting its legitimacy on grounds of age, but the horse had been allowed to continue racing. These objections were aired again before the Derby and following the race a legal case was brought before a court to settle the matter. During the trial the judge had ordered Running Rein to be produced so that it could be examined by a vet and its real age determined. The owners produced excuse after excuse – but no horse. If it had been produced, the game would have been up. Running Rein was in fact Maccabeus – a three year old, which had been bought by a gambler called Abraham Levi, who appropriately also went by a different name, Goodman.

The case saw the race awarded to second-placed horse Orlando. The judge, Baron Alderson, said in his concluding statement: 'If gentlemen would associate with gentlemen, and race with gentlemen, we should have no such practices. But, if gentlemen will condescend to race with blackguards they must expect to be cheated.'

Levi/Goodman was banned from racing by the Jockey Club and disappeared over the English Channel to France. He would have made £50,000 from the attempted scam.

The scandal of the Derby of 1844 was not limited to one horse. Two others, The Ugly Buck and Ratan, were allegedly doped, and Leander was also believed to be overage but he was destroyed after his leg was broken during the race by another horse – Running Rein.

NO WIN GWYNNE

In the Aintree Grand National of 1849, The Knight of Gwynne was being ridden by Captain D'Arcy. As they approached the finish they were a distant second to Peter Simple, ridden by Tommy Cunningham. D'Arcy – who'd bet a lot of money on his horse – began to offer bribes to Cunningham as they neared the finishing line. He started at £1,000 and this was increased – as his chances of winning decreased – to £4,000. Cunningham continued on to win the race. Captain D'Arcy might have been better off betting on Peter Simple, whose starting price was 20/1 against his nag's 8/1. The fate of the bold Captain D'Arcy is not known, although he is recorded as not having raced again in the National.

DRAWN TEST MATCH

At the end of the 1897–8 English football season, a series of test matches were played to decide relegation and promotion. Stoke had finished bottom of the First Division, below Blackburn Rovers on goal difference. These two teams were put up against Newcastle United and Burnley from the Second Division.

By the time Burnley came to Stoke's Victoria Ground, both sides had the same number of points. A draw would see both in the First Division. And that's what happened. A game that had no shots at goals. Players would aim their kicks so wide the corner flags were in more danger of being hit than the back of the net. The crowd of 4,000 were not pleased at this non-football match and subjected the players to barracking, but the game ended as it had begun – with a 0–0 draw.

Newcastle had beaten Blackburn 4–0 but any acrimony over the played-out draw at Stoke was rendered moot as the First Division was expanded from 16 clubs to 18, and Newcastle and Blackburn joined the upper division.

Following these games, test matches were abandoned and promotion and relegation was carried out automatically according to final league positions.

BILLY, DON'T BE A HERO

Billy Meredith was a superstar of early twentieth-century football. Born in July 1874, he was a Welsh international and played the majority of his early career at Manchester City. He captained them to their first FA Cup win in 1904. Meredith was famous for playing with a toothpick in his mouth, which he claimed helped his concentration. He was a winger who could also score goals.

In the 1904–5 season his club were vying with Newcastle United for the league title. Both sides had the same number of points as they approached the last game of the season. On 29 April 1905, City were away to Aston Villa, a game they lost 3–2, thus denying them any chance of the league title. During the game a punch-up between the Villa captain Alex Leake and City player Sandy Turnbull became the subject of a Football Association inquiry. When it was published in August, the investigation sensationally concluded that Meredith had offered a bribe: £10 to Alex Leake to lose the game.

Meredith was banned for a season. He protested his innocence, saying, 'I am entirely innocent and am suffering for others. Such an allegation as that of bribery is preposterous!' Meredith had not been permitted to give evidence and Leake admitted Meredith's suggestion might have been a joke.

As a result, Meredith faced a year without any income from football. He was under the impression his club would look after him, but no money was forthcoming, as City were under close scrutiny.

Meredith said he was only acting on the instructions of the club's manager Tom Maley. Furthermore, he revealed that the club had been paying more than the maximum wage permitted for players (£4 a week) through bonus payments. Investigations found irregularities in the accounts of the club, such as non-existent players being paid, and that secret bank accounts had been used to make the payments.

This led to the club losing its chairman, its board, its manager and 17 players, who were all given bans. The FA ordered the players to be sold and they were put up for auction. Meredith was one of them. With three others from City he joined the club's rivals, Manchester United. On his first game for his new club on 1 January 1907 he scored. The opposition? Aston Villa. Meredith went on to become a United favourite, where he was known as the Welsh Wizard. He was in the side that won United's first league championship in 1908.

A keen proponent of players' rights, he was actively involved in the formation of the Players' Union. He later rejoined Manchester City after a dispute over money with United and played on until retiring in 1924, aged 49. He'd played 1,568 games.

BAD FRIDAY

Football matches between Manchester United and Liverpool are competitive affairs, with both sides keen to emerge the victor and gain the bragging rights. Unusually, the rivalry is greater than when they play derby matches against clubs from their respective cities. However, on Good Friday 1915 things were not quite as competitive as they might have been.

Manchester United went ahead 1–0 late in the first half. In the second half, when they were awarded a penalty, United's Patrick O'Connell came up to take it. He wasn't the normal penalty taker and it was easy to see why: his attempt was directed so far wide of the goal that it almost hit the corner flag. He seemed to be smiling afterwards. Fans looked on bemused – what was going on?

When Liverpool's Fred Pagnam directed a header that hit the crossbar, his teammates were seen to gesticulate angrily towards him. A second goal for the home side came in the second half and the game drifted to its end.

Rumours abounded of players from both teams being seen, in the days leading up to the match, meeting in pubs and discussing the game's outcome. During the game itself there were reports that the Manchester United manager had left the stadium early. Players were heard arguing at half-time in their dressing room. Bookmakers were suspicious at the large number of bets that had been placed on a 2–0 result at odds of 7–1. What was behind it all?

It was simple: players on both sides had arranged beforehand to make sure the result was a 2–0 home win for Manchester, with a goal in each half; this would help ensure they were not relegated.

A Football Association inquiry announced: 'It is proved that a considerable sum of money changed hands by betting on the match, and that some of the players profited thereby. By their action they have sought to undermine the whole fabric of the game and discredit its honesty and fairness.'

Seven of the players from the game were banned for life:

Liverpool	Manchester United
Jackie Sheldon	Sandy Turnbull
Tom Miller	Arthur Whalley
Bob Pursell	Enoch 'Knocker' West
Thomas Fairfoul	

West protested his innocence and sued the Football Association twice for libel. He offered to donate £50 to charity if anyone could prove he was guilty. The others who had been banned all joined the armed forces, as league football had been halted while the First World War continued. One of the players, Sandy Turnbull, was killed at Arras in 1917. The other players had their bans rescinded in 1919 in recognition of their war service.

BLACK SOX

Hooray for the clean Sox!

Cry heard in courtroom, 2 August 1921

What happened at baseball's World Series of 1919 remains one of the most infamous sporting scandals. The nine-match series was played between the Chicago White Sox and the Cincinnati Reds. The White Sox were the favourites to win, but rumours that a 'fix' was to take place started spreading before the first pitch was thrown.

The White Sox were owned by Charles Comiskey, who, like most other owners of the time, did not pay his players highly. His reluctance to even spend money on cleaning the uniforms led to the team being nicknamed the Black Sox.

Despite the scandal's high profile, much of the detail is still not clear, including the motivation behind the fix. Some believe the players were fed up of being poorly paid by Comiskey and wanted to get their own back. Others suggest it was just a way of supplementing their income.

The idea of the fix possibly originated from White Sox player Arnold 'Chick' Gandil or from professional gambler 'Sport' Sullivan. Gandil recruited some of his teammates, including Eddie Cicotte, the team's best pitcher. Another was the best hitter, 'Shoeless' Joe Jackson.

The players met in a New York hotel on 21 September 1919, ten days before the series began. They agreed to carry out the match-fixing – for $80,000. Then they received another offer – for $100,000 – from another gambler, 'Sleepy' Bill Burns, working with an associate called Billy Maharg, an ex-boxer. Burns and Maharg met with New York crime boss Arnold Rothstein, who had the finances to fund the venture. Whether Rothstein did or did not fund the fix is another element that remains unclear. He is known to have bet heavily on the Cincinnati Reds winning.

The Games

Game 1

On 1 October 1919, the World Series began. White Sox pitcher Eddie Cicotte indicated to the plot's backers that they were going to carry out the fix by hitting one of the Reds' players in the back with one of his pitches. Cicotte had been paid $10,000 the night before.

The Reds won the game 9–1.

Game 2

The White Sox lost again, this time 4–2.

Game 3

White Sox pitcher Dickie Kerr was not part of the fix and the Reds didn't score one run. The White Sox won 3–0.

Game 4

Cicotte was back pitching. He made several errors that shocked the home crowd – this was the second game being played at Comiskey Park, the White Sox stadium. The Reds now went 3–1 ahead in the series. A sum of $20,000 was received by those who were in on the scheme, adding to the $10,000 they had received after Game 2.

Game 5

A 5–0 win for the Reds put them 4–1 up and needing just one more win to secure the title. After the game the White Sox players were annoyed that they weren't seeing all the money they'd been promised, so they resolved to play to win.

Game 6

The White Sox were 4–0 down before fighting back to tie at 4–4 by the start of the seventh innings. In the tenth innings the White Sox were able to secure the run that won them the game 5–4.

Game 7

The Reds made errors and the White Sox got themselves into a 4–0 lead, which they defended, only losing one run, to run out 4–1 winners. The series was now 4–3 to the Reds.

Game 8

White Sox pitcher 'Lefty' Williams played badly. There were suggestions he had been told before the game his wife was in danger unless he played poorly. Williams was replaced as the Reds went 5–0 ahead after just two innings and ran out 10–5 winners. The Cincinnati Reds had won the World Series.

Grand Jury

In September 1920 an investigation began into match-fixing claims and Cicotte and Jackson admitted their involvement. A possibly apocryphal story has it that when Jackson left the courthouse, a boy said to him, 'It ain't so, Joe, is it?' To which the player replied, 'Yes, kid, I'm afraid it is.' A grand jury indicted several gamblers and eight players on charges of conspiracy to defraud. The players were:

- Eddie Cicotte

- Oscar 'Happy' Felsch

- Arnold 'Chick' Gandil

- 'Shoeless' Joe Jackson

- Fred McMullin

- Charles 'Swede' Risberg

- George 'Buck' Weaver

- Claude 'Lefty' Williams

The Trial

The trial began on 18 July 1921. The players' confessions had mysteriously disappeared before the trial started and on 2 August all players were found not guilty. When the verdict was given, the Cook County courtroom erupted in celebrations, with bailiffs joining in the cheering. Judge Hugo M. Friend was seen smiling at the outcome, which he called 'a just verdict'. The players were carried from the courtroom on the jurors' shoulders.

Landis

Following the trial, the need to ensure the sport's integrity resulted in the creation of a Commissioner of Baseball. The man who was the first to be appointed to this all-powerful post was Judge Kenesaw Mountain Landis. He wasted no time: the eight 'Black Sox' were banned from the sport for life. Landis issued a statement that read:

Regardless of the verdict of juries, no player that throws a ball game, no player that entertains

> *proposals or promises to throw a game, no player that sits in a conference with a bunch of crooked players and gamblers where the ways and means of throwing games are discussed, and does not promptly tell his club about it, will ever play professional baseball.*

None of them ever did again.

BULL STEERED BY FOX

Middleweight boxer Jake LaMotta was known as 'The Bronx Bull' for his pugnacious style of fighting. He was the first man to beat the great Sugar Ray Robinson, whom he fought six times.

On 14 November 1947, LaMotta fought Billy Fox at New York's Madison Square Garden. Fox was the underdog and there were long odds on him winning, something that was of great importance to figures from the crime world.

After four rounds, Fox was declared the winner. LaMotta hadn't performed with any of his usual aggression. What was going on?

There were immediate suspicions about the fixing of this fight and both boxers' purses were kept back until the fight was investigated. LaMotta explained his poor and unaggressive performance in the ring as being down to an injury to his spleen. He was fined $1,000 and suspended for seven months for not informing the boxing authorities of his injury.

It took until 1960 for the truth to come out when LaMotta admitted publicly to throwing the fight for the Mafia. He did so in order to secure a bout for the world middleweight title, which he subsequently won in 1949, beating Frenchman Marcel Cerdan.

LaMotta's story was later made into the 1980 Hollywood movie *Raging Bull* directed by Martin Scorsese and starring Robert De Niro as LaMotta.

SPA FOR THE COURSE

At the Spa Selling Plate at Bath on 16 July 1953, the French horse Francasal came home the winner, at 10/1. A lot of money had been bet on the horse and normally this would have seen a reduction in the odds, but word was not passed to the on-course bookmakers as somehow the course's telephone lines had been cut before the race.

It would be wrong to give Francasal any of the credit for the win as the horse that crossed the line first was actually called Santa Amaro. The swap was performed as part of a scam called a 'ring-in', where a poor horse is secretly replaced by a better one.

Those responsible were eventually tracked down and a criminal case saw prison sentences handed out at the Old Bailey. It was estimated that £1 million had been won – or lost, depending on which side of the fence you were on.

LAYNE DOWN BETS

The Biggest Sports Scandal of the Century
Sunday People, 12 April 1964

Peter Swan and Tony Kay were England football internationals who played for club side Sheffield Wednesday. Swan was a tough centre-back and Kay a wing-half. In December 1962 they had an away fixture at Ipswich, a game that they had struggled to win in the past.

Before the match they were approached by teammate David Layne, who suggested they could make some money by betting on the match result. All three each gave £50 to Jimmy Gauld, an ex-teammate of Layne's, to wager on their team losing. The odds were 2/1.

Gauld had also set up similar schemes for the Lincoln v Brentford and Oldham v York games the same day.

Sheffield Wednesday were duly beaten 2–0 by Ipswich, as the players had expected. Kay was the *Sunday People*'s Man of the Match. Lincoln lost 3–1 and York lost 3–2. All three matches had ended with the 'right' result. It was reported that bookmakers lost £35,000.

The story broke when Jimmy Gauld sold his story to the *Sunday People* newspaper. His account, which implicated Swan, Kay and Layne, came out in April 1964 and caused outrage. The Sheffield Wednesday chairman Andrew Stephen said to reporters in the immediate aftermath of the story breaking: 'I'm too stunned and shocked to say anything much at the moment.'

Convicted in 1965, Gauld was ordered to pay £5,000 costs and was jailed for four years. (He had won £3,275 and received £7,240 from the *Sunday People*.) As he was sentenced the judge said to him:

Over a long period and from one end of this kingdom to another you have befouled professional football and corrupted your friends and acquaintances. You have done it in order to put money into your own pocket.

Over the years football fans have paid their shillings to see a football match played, as they thought, by experts. For those shillings, they got not a match, but a dishonest charade.

Swan, Kay and Layne were each jailed for four months for conspiracy to defraud and were banned from football for life. They couldn't watch games, or even play in pub team matches. Kay had been transferred to Everton not long after the Ipswich game for a £60,000 transfer fee – making him Britain's most expensive player, and the Merseyside club lost the services of a player who had not been doing anything untoward in an Everton jersey.

Six other players who were involved in other fixed games were also given jail sentences at the same trial:

- Brian Phillips (former captain, Mansfield Town): 15 months

- Ken Thomson (Hartlepool United): 6 months

- Jack Fountain (former captain, York City): 15 months, 50 guineas costs

- Dick Beattie (St Mirren): 9 months

- Sammy Chapman (former captain, Mansfield Town): 6 months

- Ron Howells (Walsall): 6 months, £100 costs

Swan's ban was lifted after eight years and he pulled on the Sheffield Wednesday jersey again. He received a warm welcome on running on to the Hillsborough pitch for his first home match.

He said afterwards, 'The only thing I had done – and I knew I had done it and done wrong – was the bet.'

FC PERJURY

Horst-Gregorio Canellas was president of German football team Kickers Offenbach. His team had gained promotion to the Bundesliga in 1970, from the second tier of German football. They spent only one year in the top flight, being relegated at the end of the season, in June 1971. They lost their place by one goal in the goal-difference column.

On 6 June 1971 – a day after his team had been relegated – Canellas was hosting his fiftieth birthday party. Among the league's officials and media guests was the national team coach Helmut Schön.

As the season neared its end, Canellas had suspected there was more to his team's decline than purely football reasons and had begun his own investigations. He had arranged the recording of phone conversations and when he replayed these to his guests at the party, it unleashed a mighty scandal.

Offenbach had been relegated with Rot-Weiss Essen, but their rivals in the relegation dogfight, Rot-Weiss Oberhausen and Arminia Bielefeld, had survived the drop. All teams had been desperate to avoid relegation as the amount of income would drop severely.

On Canellas' tape, the Cologne and national team goalkeeper, Manfred Manglitz, was heard saying that when his team played Rot-Weiss Essen he would let goals go in past him. His fee? Twenty-five thousand Deutschmarks.

Canellas had put himself in the conspiracy by attempting to entrap players. He offered 140,000 Deutschmarks to Hertha Berlin players to ensure victory over Arminia Bielefeld. It turned out that one of the Hertha Berlin players had already been offered money to lose that game by Bielefeld and took that option, as they had offered more money! Hertha had not lost a home game – until they lost the final one against Bielefeld.

The scandal grew and grew until it was discovered that 18 games affecting the relegation-zone clubs had been subject to match-fixing. Sixty players from ten clubs were identified as being involved.

One of the teams was FC Schalke 04 whose players had accepted money to lose a game to Arminia Bielefeld. When questioned they denied any wrongdoing. When it was proved they had lied, and committed perjury, their team gained the derogatory nickname FC *Meineid* – 'FC Perjury'.

The scandal had an effect on the game in Germany as attendances fell, with fans turning their backs on the discredited league. It was only with West Germany's victory in the 1974 World Cup, held in West Germany, that the game was rejuvenated in the country.

GIVE THEM A GOOD HAND

Eyebrows were raised when at a horse race for two-year-olds at Leicester on 29 March 1982 Flockton Grey came home 20 lengths in front of the second-placed horse. This impressive form wasn't reflected in its odds of 10/1 so something unusual seemed to have taken place. It transpired that Flockton Grey wasn't Flockton Grey at all, but was in fact a horse called Good

Hand. Good Hand was three years old, giving it a distinct advantage. The horse's owner, Ken Richardson, was 'warned off', i.e. banned from racing by the Jockey Club for 25 years. He later took over Doncaster Rovers Football Club and was jailed for arranging the attempted arson of the club's ground.

LOAD OF HRUBESCH

In the 1982 World Cup held in Spain, Algeria were in a group alongside West Germany, Austria and Chile. The Germans were confident of winning their first game against Algeria, but their overconfidence was misplaced, and they lost 2–1.

The Algerians lost to Austria 2–0 in their next game but in their last game they beat Chile 3–2. Their progress in the tournament was now dependent on a favourable result from the West Germany v Austria game, which was played the day after their own final group game.

Algeria sat second in the group, below Austria and above West Germany. To be the first African nation to progress to the next stages of a World Cup they required an Austria win, or a West Germany win by more than two goals, as this would give Algeria a better goal difference than Austria and they would go through with West Germany. If West Germany won by one or two goals then both West Germany and Austria would go through.

In the game, West Germany's Horst Hrubesch scored in the tenth minute. Both teams then did nothing. The game continued as a kickabout, with no team attempting to score again. The disgusted Algerian fans burnt banknotes at what seemed like a conspiracy. Although it suited both teams, there was outrage in both Germany and Austria, summed up by one German commentator who said, 'What is happening here is disgraceful and has nothing to do with football.'

The game was given various titles: the 'Disgrace of Gijón', the 'Shame of Gijón' and, harking back to events before World War Two, '*El Anschluss*' – referring to the annexation of Austria by Germany in 1938. No conspiracy to collude was ever proven.

West Germany reached the final but were beaten by Italy. Due to the outcry, the format of the group stages was changed and the last games were all played on the same day, at the same time.

FINE COTTON TRADING

In 1982 an Australian conman called John Gillespie had attempted a 'ring-in' at a horse race, but the attempt had failed. This did not deter him from trying again. While in prison he found his cellmate's brother was a horse trainer called Hayden Haitana.

Once out of prison, Gillespie recruited Haitana and for the 'good horse' part of the scheme bought one called Dashing Solitaire. The 'poor horse', called Fine Cotton, was then acquired. Fine Cotton was run in a few races to set up its form, ready for it to be replaced at a specific race, the Commerce Novice Handicap at Eagle Farm racecourse in Brisbane.

The plan began to unravel when Dashing Solitaire went lame and another horse had to be quickly procured. This was Bold Personality, a horse with decent form. The only problem it presented was it didn't look very much like Fine Cotton, so hair dye was liberally applied to try to match its colouring. The schemers had forgotten to replicate the distinctive white markings on Fine Cotton's legs so paint was applied. It didn't look too convincing, though, so bandages were applied to cover up the mess.

On 18 August 1984 – race day – the starting odds for 'Fine Cotton' were 33/1. But with the large amount of betting taking place – word was starting to get round about the scam – the price fell to 7/2. The racing authorities were alerted and when 'Fine Cotton' romped home the game was up.

Haitana fled but was later caught and jailed for six months. He was banned from any racecourse for life, but the ban was eventually lifted in 2013.

The brains behind the scheme, John Gillespie, was also jailed. He later claimed it was all a ruse, that the scheme was devised in order to make money by betting on the horse that came second – and was ultimately awarded the victory, Harbour Gold, but this was ridiculed by racing officials.

FIDALING WHILE ROME BURNS

The 1987 World Athletics Championships were held in Rome's Stadio Olimpico. In the long jump competition Carl Lewis took gold, Robert Emmiyan of the USSR the silver and Italian athlete Giovanni Evangelisti received the bronze medal, after jumping 27 feet 6 inches (8.38m), beating the American Larry Myricks by 2 inches.

The trouble was, Evangelisti hadn't actually jumped that far.

In March 1988 an Italian Olympic Committee investigation found that eight members of the Italian track and field federation FIDAL (Federazione Italiana Di Atletica Leggera) were implicated in giving a false measurement of the Italian's final jump. (Later investigations estimated the actual jump to be under 26 feet.) While the crowd and other athletes were distracted by a medal ceremony the judges had recorded a false distance.

One of the officials was Luciano Barra, the general secretary and assistant to Primo Nebiolo, the Italian head of athletics' governing body, the International Amateur Athletic Federation (IAAF). The officials involved were given bans from the sport. Nebiolo denied any involvement with the incident. Evangelisti had to hand back his bronze, which was awarded to the rightful winner Myricks.

VA VA VA-OM

The world of football is much more rotten than people like to think.

Christophe Robert, Valenciennes FC

On 26 May 1993, residents of the French city of Marseille celebrated as their team had just won the first ever Champions League final.

In the final held in Munich, a Basile Boli goal was enough to defeat an AC Milan with the likes of Marco van Basten, Franco Baresi and Paolo Maldini in the side.

It was the first time a French club had won the top club competition in Europe (previously the European Cup) and Olympique Marseille (known as OM) continued their successful run by securing their domestic league title a few days later. It was their fifth championship in a row. However, there was not much time to celebrate as allegations of match-fixing began to surface.

It transpired that in the domestic league championship, Marseille had bribed Valenciennes FC (VA) into losing a game against them on 20 May.

Representatives of Marseille, general manager Jean-Pierre Bernès and player Jean-Jacques Eydelie, had contacted three Valenciennes players and offered them money to underperform. One of the Valenciennes players, Jacques Glassmann, reported the bribery attempt to the referee of the game in question at half-time.

When the scandal broke, Marseille's president Bernard Tapie denied the accusations, saying: 'It's a lynching; there's not the slightest proof of guilt.' Eydelie later stated that Tapie had asked that he contact Valenciennes players he had known while at Nantes, saying: 'We don't want them acting like idiots and breaking us before the final with Milan.'

But there was proof in what became known as 'L'affaire VA-OM'. Another Valenciennes player, Christophe Robert, confessed to taking the money and showed police to a hole in his aunt's garden where he had buried the cash: 250,000 francs.

Robert and another player, Argentina's Jorge Burruchaga (who scored the winning goal in the 1986 World Cup final), were charged by the authorities.

Marseille were relegated to France's second division for the following season and stripped of their recent championship. They were thrown out of the Champions League and so couldn't defend their victory. They retained their victory in the final against AC Milan but there were doubts about their progress in the tournament. Rangers player Mark Hateley, whose club faced Marseille in the group stages, alleged that he was offered a bribe not to play against them.

The individuals involved were suspended – with the exception of Tapie. He was a minister in François Mitterand's government, but his immunity was withdrawn by a vote of French MPs and he was placed under investigation for corruption and interfering with witnesses. In May 1995 he was found guilty and given an eight-month jail sentence. Burruchaga, Robert and Eydelie were given suspended sentences.

Glassmann, who had reported the bribery, was ostracised as a result. He was booed wherever he played and called 'traitor' for his honesty.

BRUCIE BONUS

Born in South Africa in 1957, Bruce Grobbelaar served an unusual apprenticeship for a footballer, spending time as a solider in the Rhodesian army, where he took part in combat operations. After his stint in uniform he played in Canada and for Crewe Alexandra in England, before joining Liverpool as backup goalkeeper to Ray Clemence in March 1981. When Clemence moved to Tottenham Hotspur, Grobbelaar became the first-choice keeper. He was between the sticks in one of the club's most successful periods. He won:

- 6 league titles

- 3 FA Cups

- 3 League Cups

- 1 UEFA European Cup

- 1 UEFA Super Cup

It was in the European Cup final of 1984 against Roma that he gained notoriety – or plaudits (depending on which team you supported) – when during a penalty shoot-out he indulged in what some regarded as gamesmanship. As the Italian players prepared to take their kicks, Grobbelaar wobbled on the goal line, on legs seemingly turned to jelly. His antics put them off and an Alan Kennedy kick won the Merseyside club their fourth European Cup.

In his 14 full seasons at Liverpool he played in the first team 627 times. This included a consecutive run of 310 appearances. He left in 1994 and played for a succession of lower-league clubs. It was in that year that *The Sun* newspaper printed allegations he had taken bribes to fix matches. The goalkeeper had been videotaped admitting that previous matches had been fixed and accepting £2,000 as an inducement for fixing future games. He was filmed talking about receiving £40,000 in connection with a Liverpool v Newcastle game in November 1993, in which the Liverpool club lost 3–0. *The Times* match report for this game reported that at the end of the game 'Bruce Grobbelaar, who had risked his knee only ten days after exploratory surgery, ran to the centre circle, embraced Andy Cole, and raised his own arm in unison with that of the spectators.' Cole had scored all three Newcastle goals. The *Guardian* called the game a 'rare and humiliating thrashing'. *The Sun* also printed claims that another game worth £125,000 to Grobbelaar ended in a 3–3 draw after he accidentally saved a shot with his foot when diving the other way.

Grobbelaar was charged with conspiracy to corrupt, along with former Wimbledon striker John Fashanu, goalkeeper

Hans Segers and Malaysian businessman Richard Lim. Grobbelaar claimed that he had only gone along with the match-fixing in order to collect evidence on those paying the bribes. After the jury were unable to agree a verdict in the first trial, a retrial saw them all acquitted.

Grobbelaar then sued *The Sun* for libel. He won and in July 1999 was awarded £85,000. The newspaper appealed and the Court of Appeal then overturned this decision, calling it an 'affront and a miscarriage of justice'.

The legal battle was not over and in 2002 the law lords overturned the Court of Appeal's decision. They accepted he had been libelled, in that there was no proof he had thrown games, but that he had accepted bribes. Grobbelaar was awarded £1 in damages and had to pay *The Sun*'s costs, estimated to be £1 million pounds. He was subsequently declared bankrupt.

Lord Bingham said: 'He had in fact acted in a way in which no decent or honest footballer would act, and in a way which could, if not exposed and stamped on, undermine the integrity of a game which earns the loyalty and support of millions. It would be an affront to justice if a court of law were to award substantial damages to a man shown to have acted in such flagrant breach of his legal and moral obligations.'

LIGHTS OUT!

A sweet strike from the right boot of Frank Lampard…
on whom the lights have just gone out.

Jon Champion, TV commentator, 3 November 1997

Lampard's goal came in a match played between West Ham United and Crystal Palace at West Ham's Upton Park.

Crystal Palace had gone 2–0 up before being pegged back to 2–2, Lampard's 20-yard strike in the sixty-fifth minute being the equaliser. As the West Ham players celebrated, the floodlights went out. They came back on, only to be extinguished again. Referee David Elleray abandoned the match after half an hour.

The following month at Selhurst Park a Wimbledon v Arsenal game experienced the same, with the lights going out seconds into the second half. The score was 0–0 at the time. Efforts to bring the floodlights back on failed. Wimbledon's director Sam Hammam said: 'This shouldn't be happening. Once was bad enough, the second wasn't pretty, and this is getting near a disaster. Unless we stop it there will be shame on the game. We are all embarrassed by it.'

As Charlton were about to face Liverpool in February 1999, a circuit-breaker device was found at The Valley, Charlton's ground. Investigations found that a security guard had been paid £20,000 to allow men from a syndicate access to install their equipment in the ground's power room to switch off the lights. The plan was rumbled when the guard's colleague informed the police.

Four men were charged: Wai Yuen Liu, who had links to a Triad crime gang and an illegal betting syndicate in Hong Kong; Charlton's security guard Roger Firth; and Malaysians Eng Hwa Lim and Chee Kew Ong. All were given jail sentences; Ong and Lim were given four years, Liu was given two and a half years and Firth one and a half years.

Gambling on Premiership matches in Asia was big business, with millions of pounds at stake on individual games. Under the rules of gambling, if a match was abandoned after half-time, the result stood and so gambling syndicates could fix the match whenever the appropriate score was reached.

JOHN THE BOOKMAKER

Australian Shane Warne is regarded as one of cricket's best ever bowlers. He played his first Test match in 1992 and his last in 2007, when Australia completed a 5–0 whitewash of England. He played in 145 Test matches and was the first player to take 600 and then 700 Test wickets.

Warne gained huge attention with his very first bowl against England in Test cricket when he bowled out Mike Gatting with 'the most beautiful delivery' as described by commentator Richie Benaud. The 'Ball of the Century' was in the first Ashes Test of 1993 and announced Warne's mastery of leg-spin bowling. Australia went on to win the series 4–1.

In 1998 it was revealed that Warne and fellow Australian player Mark Waugh had been involved in giving information to an illegal bookmaker. Starting in September 1994, they had supplied a figure known as 'John the Bookmaker' with details of the condition of the pitch and weather for upcoming games. They hadn't passed on information on team selection.

While the scandal was revealed in 1998, the story had been kept quiet for several years, with the players secretly fined by the Australian Cricket Board in 1995. That year Warne, Waugh and fellow Australian player Tim May had all accused Pakistani player Saleem Malik of offering them money to fix a Test match between their two countries in September 1994. Warne and Waugh admitted they had been 'naive and stupid' to pass on information – their reputation and credibility were badly affected by the affair.

CRONJE-ISM

South African captain Hansie Cronje is a man of enormous integrity and honesty.

United Cricket Board of South Africa press statement, 7 April 2000

Some sportsmen and women become so famous they are known beyond their sport – household names like movie stars. Hansie Cronje reached that level of fame in South Africa, which made his fall even harder.

He had played rugby and cricket at school before becoming a professional cricketer. He was good enough to be the captain of his country's team when aged just 24. His record as captain was good, leading them to 27 Test wins out of 53, and 99 out of the 138 One Day Internationals he was in charge for.

His image as the upright captain was to be shattered in April 2000 when a match-fixing scandal broke. Indian police had told the South African cricket authorities that they had a tape recording of Cronje discussing match-fixing with an Indian bookmaker. He denied the allegations initially but eventually admitted that he hadn't been 'entirely honest'.

The King Commission was set up to investigate the allegations. It heard that Cronje had been involved in taking money in return for information on upcoming games. As well as this he had also tried to involve his teammates in activities beyond mere passing of information. Before a benefit game in India in December 1996 he had offered his teammates money if they underperformed. The proposal was discussed, but rejected. Further evidence and admissions led to him being banned from cricket for life in October 2000.

With cricket no longer his source of income, he started working at a company making earth-moving equipment. When returning from work one Friday night in June 2002, the aircraft taking him from Johannesburg to his home east of Cape Town flew into a mountain and he died. Since his death, rumours have arisen that it wasn't a straightforward aviation accident but that shadowy figures were behind it, figures who wanted to make sure Cronje was unable to reveal anything further.

While testifying at the King Commission, he had said: 'I can't tell you the shame this whole affair has caused me', which he put down to his 'unfortunate love of money'.

Cronje had 72 bank accounts in the Cayman Islands, and he admitted that he had taken at least $130,000 – and a leather jacket for his wife – from bookmakers in the years 1996 to 2000.

BATTING OUT OF ORDER

Mohammad Azharuddin was an Indian batsman who played for his country between 1984 and 2000. He was captain during most of the 1990s and was the most successful, with a record of 90 wins from 174 matches, before this record was superseded by Mahendra Singh Dhoni.

Azharuddin played in 99 Test matches and 334 One Day Internationals for India, and was regarded as one of the most stylish of batsmen, adept at playing shots with his wrists. He started his Test career with three centuries in three matches – a record that still stands.

In December 2000, when South African cricket captain Hansie Cronje was being investigated over taking bribes to fix matches, he stated that he had been introduced by Azharuddin to an illegal bookmaker from Delhi called Mukesh Gupta, known as MK and also as 'John the Bookmaker' – the same man who had been involved in Shane Warne and Mark Waugh's spot of bother.

The Indian Central Bureau of Investigation looked into the affair and was able to secure the cooperation of Gupta. The report stated that Azharuddin had admitted fixing three One Day Internationals (although he later denied doing so):

- India v South Africa (Titan Cup 1996)

- India v Sri Lanka (Pepsi Asia Cup 1997)

- India v Pakistan (Pepsi Asia Cup 1999)

Gupta was said to be behind the fixing of the matches in 1996 and 1997, while the third was alleged to have been organised by another bookmaker. Azharuddin was reportedly paid £150,000 by Gupta.

Azharuddin was given a life ban from the sport by the Board of Control for Cricket in India. Other Indian players received punishments for their involvement: Ajay Sharma was also banned for life, and Manoj Prabhakar and Ajay Jadeja were each given a five-year ban.

Azharuddin later served in the Indian Parliament: he became a Member of Parliament for Moradabad in 2009, but lost his seat in the 2014 elections. In 2012, his ban had been lifted by an Indian high court. A movie biopic of his life, called *Azhar*, was released in May 2016.

KOREA OPPORTUNITIES

The 2002 World Cup was jointly hosted by South Korea and Japan, and it was felt by some teams that there was evidence one of the host nations was assisted in progressing through the tournament.

It was an event of upsets and unusual results. World Cup holders France went out in the group stages without scoring a goal and Argentina went out early. Unfancied Turkey made it to the semi-finals, but it was another team who, in reaching the semi-finals, raised a few eyebrows.

Both host countries made it out of the group stages safely but Japan were then eliminated in their first knockout game by Turkey. At the same stage, South Korea's opponents were Italy, who had a strong team with players such as Fabio Cannavaro, Alessandro Del Piero, Christian Vieri, Filippo Inzaghi, Francesco Totti and Alessandro Nesta. They were captained by elegant defender Paolo Maldini and the man in goal was Gigi Buffon.

South Korea v Italy, 18 June 2002

Time	South Korea	Italy	Score
4th minute	Awarded penalty.	Saved by Buffon.	0–0
18th minute		Italy score, through Christian Vieri.	0–1

Time	South Korea	Italy	Score
88th minute	Goal by Seol Ki-hyeon.		1–1
103rd minute (extra time)		Francesco Totti fouled in penalty box. Despite there being contact, was booked for diving and, as a second yellow card, was sent off.	1–1
110th minute		Damiano Tommasi scores a 'golden goal'. Goal is chalked off for offside.	1–1
117th minute	Ahn Jung-hwan scores a header. Korea win on 'golden goal'.		2–1

The Italian newspapers summed up the national feeling with headlines like 'Shame!' (*Gazzetto dello Sport*) and 'Thieves!' (*Corriere dello Sport*). An Italian government minister, Franco Frattini, said: 'The referee was a disgrace, absolutely scandalous.'

Was there a conspiracy to expel the Italians? Some bad decisions were made throughout the match but Italy were not blameless. Although it didn't result in a goal, the fourth-minute penalty was awarded because Italian defenders were seen grabbing on to their opponents. And for South Korea's equaliser, the opportunity was only presented to striker Seol Ki-hyeon when Christian Panucci lost the ball in his own penalty box. Christian Vieri missed a glorious close-range chance when the game was 1–1 and Rino Gattuso also missed a good chance.

Whatever the reality, the Italians felt cheated. Some observers felt there was a conspiracy to keep one of the host teams in the tournament (in order to maintain attendance numbers). These feelings would only be increased after the next match.

South Korea v Spain, quarter-final, 22 June 2002

Time	South Korea	Spain	Score
49th minute		Ruben Baraja's headed goal is disallowed for pushing.	0–0
92nd minute		Fernando Morientes' goal is disallowed, the ball being judged to have crossed the line and gone out of play before it was crossed.	0–0

Time	South Korea	Spain	Score
120th minute		Spain win a corner but the referee blows full-time whistle before it can be taken.	0–0
Penalty shoot-out	5 penalties scored.	3 penalties scored.	5–3 (on penalties)

The Spanish reaction to going out was as strong as that of Italy. Spain's Iván Helguera had to be restrained after going after Egyptian referee Gamal Ghandour. Helguera said after the match: 'What happened here was robbery.' Two disputed disallowed goals was a clear sign to the Spanish and many watching that they were not going to be allowed to progress, although they had chances and the team were criticised for being too defensive tactically. South Korea became the first Asian team to reach a World Cup semi-final, but were beaten 1–0 by Germany.

Whether or not it acted as a spur, the teams that felt wronged both won the World Cup soon after: Italy in 2006 and Spain in 2010.

DODGY HOYZER

In 2005, with Germany about to host the World Cup the following year, feelings were positive about the game of football in the country. That was until one of their referees was jailed for match-fixing. The referee was Robert Hoyzer, who had connived with Croatian gambler Ante Sapina to affect the result of matches. They had met in a Berlin sports bar owned by Sapina's brother Milan.

Hoyzer's refereeing in a German Cup match in August 2004 between regional league side Paderborn and first-division team Hamburg had raised concerns. After being 2–0 down, Paderborn were awarded two suspicious penalties and Hamburg had one of their forwards, Emile Mpenza, who had scored one of their goals, sent off. Paderborn won 4–2. Ante Sapina was said to have made €750,000 from this one match.

When the concerns resulted in an investigation, Hoyzer confessed all. Further work by police revealed that players and other match officials were involved.

Hoyzer was given a 29-month jail sentence for fixing or attempting to fix nine games. Ante Sapina was jailed for 35 months and bar owner Milan received a suspended sentence of 16 months. A second referee, Dominik Marks, who had netted Ante Sapina over €800,000 for a fixed match between Karlsruhe SC and MSV Duisburg, avoided jail, receiving an 18-month suspended sentence. He had attempted to fix four matches.

A contrite Hoyzer, who had earned €67,000 and a large TV set, said: 'I'm very sorry about all the people I lied to and cheated. I've damaged German soccer greatly.'

THE WHISTLE MAFIA

Brazil is seen by many as the spiritual home of football, a country where free-flowing, attacking football is played in a carefree manner. And while this is true some of the time, there is no escaping the reality that football in Brazil is a professional game, susceptible to the same pressures anywhere else 'the beautiful game' is played.

In 2005 the darker side of football came to light when two referees were found to have fixed matches in the country's domestic leagues. Edilson Pereira de Carvalho and Paulo José Danelon were paid by businessman Nagib Fayad. Both received around £2,500 a game.

Carvalho admitted taking money from a gambling syndicate to fix matches in Brazil's first division. He claimed that he did it only as he was in debt, saying, 'I was corrupted, I was seduced, I allowed myself to get taken in by this easy money.' Carvalho was attacked by a fan of one club as he left court. The fan slapped him on the head and shouted, 'You robbed Corinthians!'

The results of 11 matches that were refereed by Carvalho were declared null and were ordered to be replayed.

Danelon admitted fixing matches in the Campeonato Paulista – the São Paulo state championship. None of the games were replayed.

Both referees were banned for life from refereeing, with Carvalho eventually finding employment as a forklift truck driver.

CALCIOPOLI SCANDAL

In the summer of 2006, Italian football fans celebrated as their captain Fabio Cannavaro lifted the World Cup. Days later, the mood changed as severe sentences were handed down to some of the country's most famous clubs:

Juventus

- Relegated (for the first time in their history) to Serie B.

- For the next season they were issued with a nine-point deduction.

- Lost their 2004–5 and 2005–6 championship titles.

- Barred from participating in the Champions League.

Lazio

- Relegated to Serie B (later rescinded).

- Had three points deducted from their next season's total.

- Barred from UEFA Cup.

Fiorentina

- Relegated to Serie B (later rescinded).

- Had 15 points deducted.

- Barred from Champions League.

AC Milan

- 30 points deducted from their 2005–6 season total.

- Eight points deducted from their next season's total.

- Barred from Champions League (later rescinded). They went on to win the 2007 Champions League final against Liverpool.

Reggina

- Lost 11 points from their next season.

What had caused these clubs to be given these punishments? The scandal, which became known as 'Calciopoli' ('Footballville') arose from recorded telephone conversations between club officials and officials of Italy's football authority, the Federazione Italiana Giuoco Calcio (FIGC). Two of Juventus' general managers, Luciano Moggi and Antonio Giraudi, were named as being at the centre of the scandal, accused of trying to arrange 'friendly' referees to officiate at their games.

Over 50 team directors, FIGC officials and referees were investigated, with many subsequently banned from participating in football. Moggi and Giraudi were given jail sentences for match-fixing but the sentences were not carried out due to the statute of limitations. Moggi said, 'Look, I'm not a saint but I've not been in the company of angels.'

IN THE FRAME

John Higgins is a four-time World Champion snooker player. But in May 2010 it wasn't his performance on the green baize that brought him widespread media attention. Rather, it was his appearance in a video which showed him apparently agreeing to lose four frames, in four matches, for £261,000.

Higgins and his manager Pat Mooney had flown to Ukraine to meet a businessman keen to work with them on events tied in with the World Series of Snooker, which comprised invitational matches that Higgins and Mooney had set up to expand snooker's popularity in countries not normally associated with the game. But the businessman known as Marcus D'Souza was actually undercover reporter Mazher Mahmood from the *News of the World* tabloid, who had set up the sting.

When the story broke, Higgins was immediately suspended and his manager Pat Mooney resigned from the board of snooker's governing body, the World Professional Snooker and Billiards Association. Higgins claimed he was 'spooked' by what he thought might be the Russian mafia and played along in order to get away and return home safely.

Higgins was cleared of match-fixing but given a six-month ban from the game and fined £75,000 for not reporting the illegal approach and for giving the impression he would breach the rules on betting. He had received no money and no match-fixing had taken place. Higgins said after the investigation, 'If I am guilty of anything it is of naivety and trusting those who, I believed, were working in the best interests of snooker and myself.'

Higgins returned to the game and in 2011 became World Champion for the fourth time.

BUTT AND NO-BALL

In October 2011 a trial took place that was unprecedented: professional cricket players facing criminal charges of corruption. The three defendants were Pakistani internationals Mohammad Amir, Mohammad Asif and Salman Butt. Alongside them was Mazhar Majeed, a UK-based agent.

Majeed had been filmed in August 2010 by undercover reporter Mazher Mahmood from the *News of the World*, posing as a representative of a gambling syndicate. On the eve of the fourth Test match against England at Lord's, Majeed had received £150,000 for arranging when two of Pakistan's bowlers would bowl no-balls the next day: for Amir, the third ball in the first over; and for Asif, the sixth ball in the tenth. Another no-ball was arranged for the second day of the match. Majeed had been filmed counting the money and saying: 'I have been fixing cricket matches constantly.' As well as the two bowlers Asif and Amir, he claimed other players were involved, including the team's captain, Butt.

All three players were suspended by the International Cricket Council (ICC). When Amir and Butt lost their appeal they lashed out at the ICC, with Amir saying, 'To me it appeared as if this is a conspiracy to defame Pakistani cricket. I am hurt and sad because we want the truth to come out.'

The chairman of the Pakistan Cricket Board, Ijaz Butt, went further and claimed England's players had taken money to lose a third One Day International between the two countries. He had to retract his inflammatory – and possibly defamatory – words in order to avoid possible legal action.

Emotions were running high and the claims alleged against the English players led to an on-field bust-up between Jonathan Trott and Wahab Riaz, who had been interviewed by police over the spot-fixing allegations. Before a One Day International at Lord's, Trott had said to Riaz: 'How much are you going to make from the bookies today?' A clash saw batting pads being thrown and Trott grabbed Riaz by the throat. They had to be separated by England's batting coach Graham Gooch.

In February 2011 the ICC banned Asif, Amir and Butt for five years, but the Pakistanis were not free of further punishment. In October 2011 they appeared at Southwark Crown Court on charges of conspiracy to cheat at gambling as well as conspiracy to accept corrupt payments. Amir and Majeed had pled guilty, and Asif and Butt were subsequently found guilty as well. They received the following jail sentences:

Butt	2 years 6 months
Asif	1 year
Amir	6 months
Majeed	2 years 8 months

The judge said: 'Whenever people look back on a surprising event in a game or a surprising result, or whenever in the future there are surprising events or results, followers of the game who have paid good money to watch it live or watch it on television will be left to wonder whether there has been fixing and whether what they have been watching is a genuine contest between bat and ball.'

Amir returned to playing cricket in March 2015, his ban being reduced for his cooperation with the ICC's anti-corruption unit. He said, 'I can't rewind those years but I should avail what time I have ahead of me.'

PERFORMANCE-ENHANCING DRUGS

Drugs are not a new phenomenon in sport. As the 1904 Olympic Marathon shows, they have been around for a long time, with athletes keen to gain an advantage over their competitors. While governing bodies have implemented measures to catch those substances deemed illegal, the pressure on the individual sportsperson to take them cannot be done away with easily.

KEY SCANDAL: THE LYING KING

The people that don't believe in cycling, the cynics, the sceptics; I'm sorry for you. I'm sorry you can't dream big and I'm sorry you don't believe in miracles.

Lance Armstrong podium speech, 2005 Tour de France

There are few fall-from-grace stories to match that of Lance Armstrong. The Texan cyclist who recovered from cancer to win seven Tour de France titles in a row became globally recognised, admired and respected for what he had achieved. When the rumours and allegations of doping became substantiated with testimony and evidence, Armstrong became hugely and publicly disgraced.

Armstrong became a professional cyclist in 1992 when he joined the Motorola team. With that team he won his first stage in the Tour de France in 1993. In October 1996 he was told he had testicular cancer, which had spread to his stomach, lungs and brain. He underwent treatment and, while given a low chance of survival, was declared cancer free in February 1997. This experience led to him founding the Livestrong charity to help those affected by cancer, which went on to eventually raise over $500 million.

Armstrong joined the US Postal Service pro cycling team and in 1998 came in fourth in the Vuelta a España. The following year he won the Tour de France. It was a sensational result and he was lauded for his achievement.

Armstrong retired from cycling in 2005 after his seventh Tour victory but returned and raced in 2009's race, finishing third. He was part of the Kazakhstan Astana team – which had been originally established to give Kazakh Alexander Vinokourov a Tour win, but this failed when he tested positive for blood doping in the Tour of 2007.

Armstrong's last Tour de France was in 2010 when he finished twenty-third following a series of crashes. He retired again from cycling in 2011.

Armstrong's performances had been suspected as being the result of performance-enhancing drugs but in the world of professional cycling it was uncommon for anyone involved to speak out: the 'code of silence' was strong. However, in 2004, someone did exactly that.

Pressure was put on Armstrong by the publication of a book, *L.A. Confidential* by Pierre Ballester and David Walsh. Walsh had been able to secure the assistance of the US

Postal Service team's soigneur (masseur and helper) Emma O'Reilly, who collaborated in what she saw as an attempt to help clean up the sport. O'Reilly, who related how Armstrong was nicknamed the Lion King, told of how in the 1999 Tour Armstrong's positive test for cortisone was explained by the team doctor backdating a prescription for a cream to treat saddle sores. Armstrong won a libel case against *The Sunday Times* when it published allegations from the book.

The allegations continued and each time Armstrong issued denials. One such was in August 2005 when French newspaper *L'Équipe* claimed that Armstrong's urine samples from 1999 had tested positive for EPO (erythropoietin, which helps produce red blood cells). Armstrong responded: 'I will simply restate what I have said many times: I have never taken performance-enhancing drugs.'

In 2010 a US federal investigation began after Floyd Landis implicated his former teammate when he revealed his own doping. The investigation was dropped in 2012 but another investigation was to prove Armstrong's undoing.

In the summer of 2012 the US Anti-Doping Agency (USADA) produced evidence of Armstrong's 'numerous anti-doping rule violations including his involvement in trafficking and administering doping products to others'. They cited his use of EPO, cortisone, testosterone and blood transfusions through the period from 1999 to 2009. Not only did he take performance-enhancing substances, he also demanded teammates followed suit. In October 2012 USADA stated: 'The evidence shows beyond any doubt that the US Postal Service pro cycling team ran the most sophisticated, professionalised and successful doping programme that sport has ever seen.'

Armstrong did not contest the findings. He was given a lifetime ban and lost all his titles, including all seven Tour de France wins. It was in his appearance on the Oprah Winfrey TV show in January 2013 that he publicly admitted his guilt for the first time. As a result of his downfall he lost his major sponsors such as Nike and was barred from working with his cancer charity.

TOM SIMPSON

Tom Simpson was the first British World Champion cyclist and the first Briton to wear the famous yellow jersey in the Tour de France, which he donned in the 1962 event. He was a high-profile figure, winning the BBC Sports Personality of the Year in 1965, but his cycling successes were to be eclipsed by his demise.

On stage 13 of 1967's Tour de France he was making the climb up the south of France's 6,200-feet-high Mont Ventoux. It was a hot day, with temperatures above 40°C. Nearing the top, Simpson was seen to weave across the road. He then fell off his bike but refused suggestions from some of his team that he abandon the race. He continued for a short distance but collapsed, unconscious, half a mile from the finish.

Simpson was declared dead soon after. The post-mortem stated he had died from a heart attack brought on by overexertion, made worse by the hot temperatures. Riders were rationed as to how much water they were allowed; Simpson had also been suffering the dehydrating effects of a stomach problem. Amphetamines and alcohol were found in his bloodstream, and he had also been carrying amphetamines in his riding jersey. Simpson's drive to compete, allied with the effects of the drugs, had kept him going when he should have abandoned the race.

Following his death, cycling's governing body, the Union Cycliste Internationale (UCI), took measures to begin formal testing of cyclists for performance-enhancing drugs.

DOWN THE TUBES

Michel Pollentier had won the Giro d'Italia in 1977 and was one of the favourites to win the following year's Tour de France. When he won the Alpe d'Huez – the famous stage of the Tour – he pulled on the yellow jersey as race leader. After reaching, literally, the highs he was about to rapidly descend and hit bottom.

After his victory, Pollentier was ordered to give a urine sample. Another rider, Antoine Gutierrez, was also chosen. Gutierrez was having trouble producing the sample and when officials investigated they found he had an apparatus featuring a tube running from a container under his armpit to his crotch. He was trying to supply a sample of someone else's urine.

Now suspicious, they ordered Pollentier to lift up his jersey – which revealed a similar arrangement. Both riders were disqualified and thrown off the Tour. Pollentier was banned for two months. He left professional cycling as a rider in 1984 and sold car tyres for a living. He also ran a cycling club for young riders. Pollentier said in 2013, 'I'm happy with my career. I gained a lot… I had some troubles too.'

POOR WULLIE

There's an expression in Scotland, 'You're not here to enjoy yourself', which reflects a Calvinistic, no-frills view of how life is to be borne and not necessarily to be filled with much fun or happiness.

This should perhaps be adopted as a motto by the Scottish national football team as this is the team who, following the Scottish penchant for invention, have come up with many ways of achieving sporting disaster, calamity and catastrophe. One such event occurred in the 1978 World Cup.

Scotland's pre-tournament preparations had lifted the hopes of its football fans, keen to see their team go further than in 1974 when they were undefeated in the group stage but still went out. The manager in 1978, Ally MacLeod, claimed they would return 'with a medal' and the departing squad were cheered around Hampden Park in an open-top bus before flying off to Argentina, where the tournament was being held. This was tempting fate.

Things didn't get off to a great start when Scotland lost their first game 3–1 to Peru and they were about to get a lot worse. Winger Willie Johnston and forward Kenny Dalglish were chosen for the post-match drugs test. Disaster was duly achieved when Johnston's came back positive. Traces of banned stimulant fencamfamine had been found in his urine.

Johnston claimed he had unknowingly taken pills to treat hay fever but his excuse was dismissed. He was sent home immediately, never to play again for his country. Scotland could have been disqualified but their quick action in punishing the player saved them from going home early. 'Scotland has taken the right measures against a player who could have done much harm to his team,' the secretary general of FIFA, Helmut Kaeser, declared. Johnston later felt he was hung out to dry by the Scottish Football Association.

The Scots hoped for a pick-me-up with their next game. They didn't get it, drawing 1–1 with Iran, who were appearing in their first World Cup.

In the last game Scotland faced the Netherlands, who had played in the 1974 final. The Scots needed to win by three clear goals to progress. They went 1–0 down after 34 minutes. But this Scotland team weren't finished yet. They upped their game and scored three, including a sensational solo effort by Archie Gemmill that remains one of the finest ever seen at a World Cup match. Unfortunately that was the end of the scoring for Scotland, but not for the Dutch. Johnny Rep blasted in a ripsnorting 25-yard piledriver only three minutes after Gemmill's wonder goal. Scotland had won, but lost.

Singer and ardent Scotland fan Rod Stewart had said after the Peru game, 'This is goodbye. It's endsville. We are out. I just can't believe it.' He was out by eight days.

SCOT FREED

Scotsman David Jenkins was a 400m runner who represented Britain at three Olympics. At the 1972 Munich games he won silver as part of the 4×400m team. He had won the 400m at the European Championships in 1971, aged just 19 years old.

Jenkins retired after the 1980 Olympics, and began researching and then passing on information to athletes on performance-enhancing drugs. This led to him working with Dan Duchaine, an American supplier of steroids. In 1988 Jenkins was arrested as part of a large-scale steroid-smuggling ring, which were bringing the drugs from Mexico into the United States.

At his trial the judge said, 'You had it all. You have brains, you have great health and a fantastic, God-given athletic ability. Then enters greed and the whole thing seems to go down the toilet bowl.' After plea bargaining, Jenkins was given seven years but was released after nine months.

While on trial, he admitted to taking steroids while he was an athlete, but as no positive test had been carried out there were no repercussions.

WHITE LANES DON'T DO IT

And Ben Johnson got a brilliant start. It's Johnson away and clear and Lewis is not going to catch him. Johnson wins it and the world record has gone again!

David Coleman, BBC commentator, 24 September 1988

The men's 100m final is one of the premier events of the Olympics such is the anticipation leading up to it. The final of the 1988 games in Seoul was of even greater interest as it brought together two competitors desperate to win: Ben Johnson of Canada and America's Carl Lewis.

Lewis had won four gold medals at the previous Olympics, held in Los Angeles in 1984, emulating Jesse Owens five decades before. One of these was for the 100m, in which Johnson came two places behind. Lewis was supremely confident, an extrovert and comfortable in the media spotlight. He was not universally loved inside the athletics world, with some feeling his showmanship could put people off. In the 1983 US National Championships at Indianapolis he won three events: the 100m, 200m and long jump. Lewis was so far in front during the 200m that for the last 10m he ran with both arms held high in celebration.

Johnson was a polar opposite. He was quiet and seemed introspective. He'd suffered with a stammer since he was 11 and had felt out of place when his family had moved from Jamaica to Canada in 1976. He was coached by Charlie Francis, who became a father figure to him. Johnson's own father had not moved with his family and had remained in Jamaica.

Johnson had been trailing Lewis: in their first eight meetings, Lewis won them all. When Lewis picked up four medals in Los Angeles in 1984, Johnson had won two: bronze in both the 100m and the 4×100m relay.

There was no love lost between the two. In a race in Seville in 1987 they had to be separated by another sprinter, Mel Lattany, as they argued after Johnson was given victory by one hundredth of a second. Lewis was sure he had won. Johnson was reported to have said to him: 'Look clown, let's run another one right now – then you'll know who won.' Following Johnson's world record-breaking sprint in 9.83 seconds at the World Championships in Rome that year, Lewis said in a TV interview: 'A lot of people have come out of nowhere and are running unbelievably, and I just don't think they're doing it without drugs.'

There was much riding on the 100m final at Seoul. After the gun, Johnson made his usual explosive start and while Lewis stayed with him, it wasn't for long. The Canadian was never behind in the race and was so comfortably in front he was able to cross the line with his index finger raised, indicating number one. Lewis was so distracted that he veered towards the edge of his own lane. Johnson's time was 9.79 seconds, a new world record. He was the fastest man in the world.

But he was not to remain there for long. His urine sample was found to contain stanozolol, an anabolic steroid. Johnson was stripped of his medal and sent home in disgrace. He also lost his World Championship title from 1987.

Johnson had started taking steroids in 1981. He told journalist Richard Moore, 'They were for training and recovery, that's all. People think I used drugs to make me run fast. A sprinter like me was born.'

Lewis was retrospectively awarded first place and Britain's Linford Christie, who had finished third, was given the silver.

Out of the eight finalists in Seoul, six were later found to be involved in doping, including Carl Lewis, who had tested positive for banned substance ephedrine during the pre-Olympics trials, but this had been kept secret at the time. He had explained it was from a herbal diet supplement and it was excused as inadvertent usage. He could have been banned for three months, thereby missing the Olympics.

Johnson said in 2013: 'I still believe I could have won the Olympic Games without any drugs back then.'

STATE PLAN 14.25

In the 1970s and 1980s the East German athletics team was successful way above its population of 17 million had any right to expect. At the 1988 Olympics, East Germany was second in the medal table, behind the Soviet Union and above the USA. East Germany's 102 medal haul was two and a half times that won by its much more populous neighbour West Germany.

After the Berlin Wall came down in 1989 the truth behind the success was revealed as documents became available showing the extent of what was a state-sponsored doping programme, known as State Plan 14.25. It was described as 'one of the largest pharmacological experiments in history' by German biologist Werner Franke.

The East Germans had given anabolic steroids – described as 'vitamin pills' – to their athletes, some as young as 11 years old. It is thought that over the 20-year period of the project, 10,000 were given performance-enhancing drugs.

One was 'Hormone Heidi' Krieger, the shot-putter who won European Championship gold in 1986. She was so affected by the changes on her body that she later had a sex-change operation, becoming Andreas Krieger in 1997. Krieger said in 2005: 'They killed Heidi.'

Krieger was just one of those who suffered long-lasting physical effects. Some of those involved had children who were born with birth defects.

Two men in charge of the programme, Manfred Ewald, head of the East German Olympic committee, and Dr Manfred Hoeppner, the chief medical officer, were given suspended sentences by German courts after facing charges of causing bodily harm in 2000.

DIEGO HOME

Argentinian footballer Diego Maradona is responsible for two abiding images of the game's World Cup. One is of him punching the ball into the goal against England in 1986 and the other came in 1994's tournament.

In 1991, while playing in Italy for Napoli, he tested positive for cocaine and was banned for 15 months by FIFA. He fled the country before facing criminal charges for possession and supply of the drug. In his absence he was fined and given a suspended prison sentence.

Back in Argentina, after a year at Valencia in Spain, he was caught with half a kilogram of cocaine but was not jailed as would be expected for a possession offence. He joined Argentinian club side Newell's Old Boys but left in 1993 after missing training. Continuing his colourful off-field behaviour, in 1994 the superstar shot at journalists with an airgun at his home in Buenos Aires.

In 1994 the World Cup was in the United States and Maradona had made a huge effort to make it into the team. He had to lose 12kg to get fit enough to play. He told the media before leaving for the USA, 'I am tired of all those who said I was fat and no longer the great Maradona. They will see the real Diego at the World Cup.'

In his country's first game, against Greece, Maradona scored and ran towards the TV cameras, and the world saw him mouth wide open and eyes bulging as he celebrated. While Maradona always celebrated his goals, this seemed especially exuberant.

There was not much else to celebrate: he was sent home after testing positive for five variants of the banned stimulant ephedrine. They were ephedrine, methylephedrine, pseudoephedrine, non-pseudoephedrine and phenylpropanolamine. Ephedrine is used by allergy and asthma sufferers, and also by those wishing to lose weight. Maradona claimed he had taken medication for a cold. He was given a 15-month ban.

IN DE BRUIN STUFF

Before 1996 Ireland was not a nation known for its success in swimming competitions. (Its swimmers' ambitions were particularly hampered by the country not having a competition-sized swimming pool.) This changed with the remarkable success of Michelle Smith in that year's Olympics in Atlanta, Georgia, USA, where she won three gold medals and a bronze, the first Irish woman to win a gold medal at an Olympics.

Smith had experienced a late surge in her career, which had raised suspicions. Three years before Atlanta, she wasn't inside the top 25. Her husband, Erik de Bruin (Smith became Smith de Bruin in 1996) was a Dutch discus thrower who had been suspended for having high levels of testosterone. He had trained Smith and it was his exercise and diet regime that was used to explain her faster times in the pool.

In 1998 Smith de Bruin was banned for four years after it was alleged that a urine sample had been tampered with alcohol. (Alcohol was often used to mask the existence of performance-enhancing drugs.) The report on her sample stated that it smelled of whisky and was 'no way compatible with human consumption'. This effectively ended her career, as she was 28 when the ban was issued. As Smith de Bruin had tested negative for drugs at the Olympics, she kept her medals. She later trained to become a barrister.

THE TOUR OF SHAME

For the scenic grandeur, physical endurance and cachet of winning, few sporting events come close to the iconic Tour de France, road cycling's most prestigious and famous championship. But no other event has been tainted with as much scandal caused by illegal practices designed to improve the performance of those taking part.

Riders taking substances to improve their performance or increase their pain tolerance have been a feature of endurance races like the Tour for many years. Strychnine, ether, amphetamines and alcohol were all taken in the past. In 1965, performance-enhancing drugs were made illegal. Like future attempts at instigating proscriptive measures, this didn't mean riders stopped taking them.

Before the 1998 Tour de France began in Dublin, a car driven by the Festina team's soigneur Willy Voet was searched by French police. They found EPO, anabolic steroids, human growth hormone and amphetamines.

The team's manager Bruno Roussel and its doctor Eric Rijckaert were arrested and then charged with drugs offences. Roussel admitted the team was fully engaged in a programme of supplying performance-enhancing substances to its riders.

Amid scenes of protest from riders who insisted on their innocence, the team was thrown out of the Tour. A stage was cancelled after cyclists protested about police interference. Five teams withdrew in protest, including all the Spanish ones. Steroids were found in the room of Italian cyclist Rodolfo Massi, who was the King of the Mountains. He became the first cyclist to be arrested for breaking anti-doping laws. Charges were later dropped.

The 1998 Tour, which was dubbed the 'Tour of Shame', saw less than a hundred riders finish the race, out of the 189 who started. It was won by Italian Marco Pantani. The following year, Pantani was thrown out of the Giro d'Italia after the haematocrit level in his blood exceeded the prescribed limit of 50 per cent. This indicated possible use of EPO.

In October 2000, French cycling star Richard Virenque finally admitted taking EPO as part of the Festina team.

SEX, DRUGS, AND TRACK AND FIELD

Of all the excuses given to explain away illegal substances found in athletes' bodies, one of the most unusual was that given by American sprinter Dennis Mitchell. Mitchell, who had won gold at the 1992 Olympics as part of the 4×100m team, and bronze in the men's 100m, tested positive for testosterone in 1998. Levels in his body were twice the allowed limit.

He claimed that these levels were due to him drinking five bottles of beer and having sex with his wife at least four times the night before the drug test – as it was her birthday. The USA Track & Field governing body accepted his reasons but the International Amateur Athletics Federation (IAAF) banned Mitchell for two years. In 2008 he admitted that his coach had injected him with human growth hormone.

MERLENE ENGINE

Jamaican-born sprinter Merlene Ottey holds several records:

- She has appeared in seven Olympics, a track and field record. Her first was Moscow in 1980 and her last was in Athens in 2004.

- She won nine Olympic medals (three silver, six bronze), the most for a track and field female athlete.

- She holds the record number of medals won at the World Championships: 14.

In August 1999 she pulled out of the World Championships after news broke of a positive test for nandrolone the previous month at a meeting in Lucerne, Switzerland. For this she was given a two-year ban. The 39 year old said the test was a 'terrible mistake' and she would prove her innocence. In November the Jamaica Amateur Athletic Association cleared their athlete and in July 2000 the IAAF followed suit, stating that her sample had not been tested properly.

While Ottey had won her fight to be able to run, she faced another one soon after – against her own teammates. At the Olympics in Sydney some of her fellow Jamaicans staged a highly unusual protest in the Olympic village, shouting 'Merlene out!' and threatening a boycott. They were unhappy at what they felt was unfairness in the selection process for the team. The 40-year-old Ottey had been selected for the 100m race in place of the younger Jamaican national champion Peta-Gaye Dowdie. Ottey had finished fourth in the national trials and so had missed out on automatic selection as only the first three were selected. Dowdie had finished first. Despite an outcry, Ottey was selected. Dowdie was said to be injured.

The protests gained attention but a stern warning from the games' organisers resulted in them being halted.

Ottey ran in the 100m but finished outside the medals in fourth place. (The gold medal went to Marion Jones but, after her later disqualification for steroid use, Ottey's fourth was upgraded to the bronze medal position.) In the 4×100m relay she was part of the team that won silver.

Ottey later ran for Slovenia, where she had set up home in 1998.

BANNED ON THE RUN

Linford Christie's ability to focus on the lane ahead, to the exclusion of everything else, helped bring him athletic glory: gold in the 100m at the 1992 Barcelona Olympics and then the following year at the World Championships. He was also European and Commonwealth 100m champion. Christie's victory in 1992 had made him the oldest Olympian champion in that event.

Christie's attempt to defend his Olympic title at the 1996 games in Atlanta failed when he false started and was disqualified. He retired in 1997 and worked in sports management and as a coach. Christie guided sprinter Darren Campbell to win silver in the men's 200m and Katharine Merry the bronze in the women's 400m at the Sydney Olympics in 2000.

Christie had been caught in controversy when he had tested positive for the banned stimulant pseudoephedrine at the 1988 Seoul Olympics. This was explained as owing to his drinking of ginseng tea and Christie avoided disqualification, albeit by a close 11–10 vote.

However, in 1999 he tested positive for the anabolic steroid nandrolone. His test showed a level 100 times above the legal amount. He had run an indoor race in Germany to show his young charges that he could still compete, but his positive test cast a shadow over his career. Aged 39, he was banned for two years by the IAAF, while UK Athletics cleared him. The British Olympic Association announced they would not provide him with accreditation for any future Olympic Games.

DRUGS CASE

Sergei Voynov was the track and field coach of the Uzbekistan Olympic team for the 2000 games in Sydney. Arriving at the Australian airport, he was caught by customs officials with 15 vials of human growth hormone in his luggage.

Voynov claimed the drugs were for his own use and not for his athletes. He said it was to treat alopecia which had caused his baldness. While in court, he showed he was bald by removing his wig. An Australian drug expert stated there was no evidence the drug was an effective treatment for his condition. Voynov was fined £4,000 for smuggling the banned substance into the country.

TULLETT TO THE JUDGE

Olga Yegorova was a Russian middle-distance runner who tested positive for EPO in July 2001. She was suspended but reinstated on a technicality and so was able to take part in the World Championships in Edmonton in Canada that year.

During the heats for the 5,000m, in which Yegorova was running, British athletes Paula Radcliffe and Hayley Tullett staged a protest, holding up a sign saying 'EPO cheats out', which they held up until security staff made them take it down. Yegorova won the race and was booed at the finish.

Radcliffe wrote later on her own website, 'Yegorova, who had been around for a while, was an 8 minutes 45 seconds runner for 3,000m who suddenly started producing times in the 8.20s. Athletes who improve a lot can be unfairly suspected of using performance-enhancing drugs, but Yegorova's progress was so startling that the questions were inevitable.'

Before the Beijing Olympics in 2008 seven Russian female athletes were given two-year bans for tampering with their urine samples. One was Yegorova.

SKIER IN THE SOUP

Saltires and Union Jacks were waved in delight on 23 January 2002 at the Salt Lake City Winter Olympics as Alain Baxter won the bronze medal in the men's slalom event – the first British skier to win an Olympic medal.

However, the flags were soon at half-mast. Baxter returned to Scotland and received a rapturous reception in his home town of Aviemore, but the next day he received a phone call from Simon Clegg, chief executive of the British Olympic Association: he had failed a drugs test, his urine showing traces of methamphetamine.

The shocked Baxter protested his innocence. He had used a Vicks inhaler but had bought it while in America, so it had different ingredients from those sold in the UK. Baxter said, 'I didn't think to check the packet. I wish I had done now.'

He was stripped of his medal but was not classified as a drugs cheat by the Court of Arbitration for Sport, which accepted he had made an innocent mistake and did not intend to gain a sporting advantage. Despite the levels of amphetamine in his body not being likely to have affected his performance, Baxter lost his appeal.

NOT IN THE CLEAR

The American company BALCO (Bay Area Laboratory Co-operative) produced an anabolic steroid called THG (tetrahydrogestrinone), also known as 'The Clear'. It was developed in secret and for good reason. There was no test in place for this drug and it was distributed to sportsmen and women in athletics, American football, baseball, boxing and cycling. A federal inquiry that began in 2002 unearthed the level of doping carried out with The Clear and the company's owner Victor Conte and its chemist Patrick Arnold were later jailed.

Among the athletes who were involved and who received subsequent bans were Americans Marion Jones and Tim Montgomery and British sprinter Dwain Chambers. Chambers' two-year ban came after a positive test for THG in 2003. He also admitted taking EPO, HGH and testosterone, spending $30,000 in one year on doping.

Chambers attempted to forge a new career in American football and English rugby league but these endeavours proved unsuccessful. He returned to athletics but faced disapproval from some high-profile athletes such as Kelly Holmes. He ran in the 2012 Olympics and reached the semi-finals of the 100m.

WARNE'S SPIN

The 2003 Cricket World Cup was the first to be played in Africa, with three countries co-hosting matches: South Africa, Kenya and Zimbabwe.

The event was not without controversy: England refused to play in Zimbabwe on 'moral, political and contractual' grounds and New Zealand refused to play in Kenya for security reasons.

But a bigger storm was caused when Australia's Shane Warne failed a drugs test and flew home. Before his team had bowled a ball, he was baling out. The Australian Sports Drugs Agency had found a drug called Moduretic in his sample. The diuretic drug was on the banned substance list because it can be used to mask steroids.

The Australian Cricket Board (ACB) stated: 'Much of Warne's evidence on these issues was unsatisfactory and the committee does not accept he was entirely truthful in his responses to questions about his knowledge of the ACB anti-doping policy.' They banned him for a year.

Warne claimed he was hard done by and a 'victim of anti-doping hysteria'. He admitted he had taken the drug, which he said he had received from his mother. He said he had taken it to look good on TV, to get rid of a double chin. In an unfortunate turn of phrase, after deciding not to appeal his banning order he was quoted as saying, 'I have decided to take the decision of the committee on the chin.'

Defending champions Australia managed to cope without their star spin bowler and won the tournament.

RIO'S OWN GOALS

Being caught with drugs in your system can have far-reaching effects on a sportsperson's career and reputation, but to miss a drugs test can be considered an offence of similar magnitude.

During training on 23 September 2003, Manchester United and England defender Rio Ferdinand was told he had been selected to give a sample for a drugs test after training was finished. He was reminded by the club's doctor but left the training ground to go shopping. When having lunch he checked his phone and saw a message from the club doctor informing him that the testers had left the training ground. Ferdinand attempted to contact the testers but was unable to do so. He took the test two days later and passed it but the fact he'd missed the original test was about to get him into deep trouble.

Ferdinand said he was preoccupied with moving house and made a simple mistake in forgetting about it, but in December 2003 he was found guilty of misconduct by the Football Association and banned for eight months and fined £50,000. The ban put him out of the European Championships the following summer. Ferdinand's punishment was compared with that given to Manchester City's Christian Negouai, who missed a drugs test the same year and was fined only £2,000. United, who were top of the league when Ferdinand began his ban, finished the season in third place behind champions Arsenal and second-placed Chelsea.

Ferdinand was no stranger to controversy, having had several driving bans for drink-driving and speeding, and for a sex tape of him, Kieron Dyer and Frank Lampard on holiday in Ayia Napa.

He was embroiled in more controversy in 2012 when he tweeted that the Chelsea and England defender Ashley Cole was 'choc ice' – a derogatory term used to suggest he was black on the outside but white on the inside. Cole had been a defence witness in the trial of teammate John Terry who had been accused of racially abusing Rio Ferdinand's younger brother Anton. Terry was cleared. Rio was cleared of being racist but was fined £45,000 by the Football Association for 'improper conduct' that brought the game into disrepute.

GREEK TRAGEDY

There was much excitement in Greece during the summer of 2004 as, for the first time in over a century, the Olympics were to be held in the country. The build-up was overshadowed, however: just before the games commenced, a drugs scandal involving the host nation's athletes erupted.

Sprinters Kostas Kenteris (who had won gold in the men's 200m at the previous games in Sydney) and Ekaterina Thanou (who had won silver in the women's 100m) were seen as having definite medal chances. Kenteris was scheduled to carry the Greek flag in the parade of athletes and was also rumoured to be the person who would light the Olympic flame in the opening ceremony.

On the eve of the games, both were selected for drug tests. They didn't turn up. Their excuse: they had been in a motorbike accident. A hospital confirmed they had been admitted and were treated for five days.

An inquiry was set up, as missing a drugs test was of course a serious offence. The duo had missed two other recent tests and they were encouraged to withdraw from the games by the International Olympic Committee. Kenteris and Thanou were banned for missing these mandatory tests.

In May 2011 both athletes were found guilty of faking the accident. They were given suspended jail sentences.

Their coach was also given a suspended sentence for perjury and also for possession of banned substances such as steroids, which had been found in his residence at the time of the crash. Six doctors at the hospital and two witnesses of the accident were also given suspended sentences. The judge said, 'The court finds that this accident never occurred.'

This was not the end of this Greek epic, however. In September 2011 a Greek appeals court overturned the May perjury verdict for both athletes, the doctors and the witnesses.

CRYSTAL SHATTERED

Waterford Crystal is a world-renowned brand. Its vases and jugs are designed to hold water, and its tumblers perhaps something a bit stronger. Sadly for the horse named after the Irish glassware company, it became known for holding something else altogether.

With rider Cián O'Connor, Waterford Crystal won the gold in the showjumping individual event at the 2004 Athens Olympics. It was Ireland's first ever equestrian medal and its only medal of the games.

Just a few months later, however, it was confirmed that the horse had tested positive for banned substances. Drugs that were normally used by humans as sedatives had been found in Waterford Crystal's urine. O'Connor pleaded innocence and his hopes on the B-sample were dashed when it went missing, believed stolen, on its way from a laboratory in France to the Horseracing Forensic Laboratory in England.

O'Connor admitted the horse had been given sedatives weeks before the games but claimed this was in relation to a fetlock injury and it was not intended to improve its performance. He said, 'I won this medal fair and square. The horse has not been given anything that would make him jump better,' but he lost his Olympic medal and was banned by the International Equestrian Federation for three months.

O'Connor went on to win bronze at the London Olympics in 2012, but the luck of the Irish deserted him in the European Championships in Germany in August 2015. The event counted towards qualifying for the 2016 Rio Olympics, yet when a member of the ground staff ran in front of him and his ironically named horse Good Luck, it led to him knocking a fence and Ireland losing out to Spain.

RAWALPINDI EXPRESS DERAILED

Pakistan fast bowler Shoaib Akhtar – known as 'the Rawalpindi Express' for his pace – was given a two-year ban from cricket in 2006 after testing positive for nandrolone. His teammate and fellow bowler Mohammad Asif had also tested positive and was given a one-year ban.

Akhtar's doctor had claimed that the 31 year old would not take any banned substance and that it was possible that nandrolone had been mixed up in herbal medicines. Both players' bans were lifted on appeal.

The two were later involved in more negative headlines in 2007 when Akhtar was given a 13-game ban for striking Asif with a cricket bat. He was fined £28,000 and sent home from the Twenty20 tournament in South Africa. He claimed he had accidentally hit his teammate when fighting with another player.

LANDIS IN TROUBLE

Floyd Landis had ridden in the US Postal Service pro cycling team with Lance Armstrong and by the 2006 Tour de France was with the Phonak Hearing Systems team.

By the start of stage 16 of that Tour, Landis was wearing the famous yellow jersey, but by the end of it his chances were gravely in doubt following a disastrous ride that saw him go from first in the general classification to eleventh. Landis said at the end, 'I had a bad day on the wrong day.'

The next day Landis started eight minutes behind the new leader. His ride that day led *Cycling News* to write, 'Without a shadow of a doubt, today will go down as one of the finest stages in modern Tour de France history.' Landis had mounted a solo attack 80 miles from the finish. Australian rider Mick Rogers summed it up by saying, 'Floyd went off like a motorbike'. The bold move saw Landis finish in overall third place, 30 seconds from the yellow jersey. The ride took him back into contention, and three days later up the Champs-Elysées to claim the title. The American was not given much time to enjoy his success as four days later a drugs test taken after stage 17 showed high levels of testosterone, almost three times above the permissible level.

Landis' Tour title was stripped from him and he was given a two-year ban. He denied taking performance-enhancing drugs but in 2010 admitted taking EPO, testosterone, HGH and also having blood transfusions during his professional cycling career. He also admitted taking insulin and female hormones. Landis said, 'The things I took, I knew what they were.'

He retired in 2011 after not being able to find a team willing to employ him.

IN THE HOUSE OF DR BLOOD

In March 2004 a newspaper interview with a former cyclist of the Spanish Kelme team, Jesús Manzano, contained allegations of systematic doping orchestrated by the team's doctor Eufemiano Fuentes.

The Spanish Guardia Civil launched an investigation called 'Operacion Puerto' and in 2006 Fuentes was arrested, along with the sporting director of the Liberty Seguros-Würth team Manolo Saiz. A raid on Fuentes' residence found numerous doses of anabolic steroids and over 200 blood bags.

Subsequent revelations in the media implicated 50 cyclists including many of the top names in the sport, some of whom later received punishments for doping:

- Alberto Contador – Liberty Seguros-Würth rider. Had won 2007, 2009 and 2010 Tours de France. Was initially cleared of involvement. Banned in 2012 for doping offences.

- Ivan Basso – Claimed not to have participated in doping but did admit to intending to. Given a two-year ban.

- Jan Ullrich – DNA samples matched that in blood bags recovered by police in the Fuentes raid. Retired in 2007. In 2012 given ban for doping. In 2013 admitted to doping with Fuentes.

- Alejandro Valverde – Was world number one in June 2010 when given a two-year ban for using EPO.

- Fränk Schleck – Paid €7,000 to Fuentes' bank account but denied doping, stating it was for advice on training

Was given a one-year ban for use of banned diuretic xipamide during 2012 Tour de France.

- Tyler Hamilton – Hamilton (who nicknamed Fuentes 'Dr Blood') stated he had worked with him to transfuse his own blood and to take EPO. When it was discovered that he had two different blood types in his blood in 2004, Hamilton claimed this could be the result of an unborn twin who died in utero. He was given a two-year ban. In 2009 he was given an eight-year ban for taking anti-depressants containing the banned substance dehydroepiandrosterone (DHEA), a hormone that converts to testosterone once inside the body.

Fuentes was given a one-year suspended jail sentence in 2013 for endangering public health. The blood bags were ordered to be destroyed by the trial judge, which brought outrage from those who were concerned about a cover-up of doping offences, not just among cyclists but footballers as well.

JONES THE DRUGS CHEAT

From a young age, American Marion Jones was marked as being destined for high achievement. She was a successful high school athlete and basketball player. When she went to university her basketball team won their national championship, but it was athletics that she chose to pursue. She missed out on the Atlanta Olympics of 1996 due to injury but made her name at the next Olympics, where she won three gold and two bronze medals in Sydney – the first woman to win five track and field medals at one Olympics:

Gold
100m
200m
4×400m relay

Bronze
4×100m relay
Long jump

To most this would be a fine achievement, but Jones had ambitiously stated she wanted to 'drive for five' golds.

At the University of North Carolina, Jones had met athletics coach C. J. Hunter and started a relationship with him; they married in 1998. Hunter became world champion shot-putter in 1999; at the same championships Jones won gold in the 100m. He was accused of taking performance-enhancing drugs and ruled himself out of competing in the 2000 Olympics, citing a knee injury. He attended Sydney as Jones' coach but during the games test results were announced that showed Hunter testing positive for nandrolone. After the couple divorced in 2002 Jones admitted the whiff of drugs surrounding her husband had affected her reputation.

Jones started a relationship with American sprinter Tim Montgomery and this resulted in them having a child together, born in June 2003. But Montgomery was implicated in the BALCO scandal (see Not in the Clear on page 90) and was subsequently banned from competition for two years.

In 2006 Jones herself failed a doping test for EPO but the second test was negative. She was cleared. However, after years of denial she finally admitted taking banned steroids in

2007. Her Olympic medals were taken away. Normally when a podium athlete is disqualified, there is upgrading of medals for those who finished behind them but this did not happen for the Sydney 100m. The athlete who won silver in Sydney was Katerina Thanou, who at the time of Jones' admission was under scrutiny for missing a mandatory drugs test before the 2004 Olympics (see Greek Tragedy on page 93). She was not awarded the gold.

Jones' fall from golden girl status saw her hit rock bottom when she was jailed for six months in January 2008 for lying to federal agents. IAAF president Lamine Diack summed things up: 'Marion Jones will be remembered as one of the biggest frauds in sporting history.'

GATLIN GONE

American sprinter Justin Gatlin won gold in the 100m at the 2004 Athens Olympics. He followed up this success with the 100m/200m double at the 2005 World Championships. In May 2006 Gatlin equalled the 100m world record, running 9.77 seconds in Doha, Qatar. It had been announced he had run in 9.76 – a new world record – but the figure had been given in error and not rounded up from the actual time of 9.766.

In 2001 he had been given a two-year ban for testing positive for amphetamine at the USA's Junior Championships. His ban was halved after a successful appeal when Gatlin stated the banned substance was due to medication he had been taking for attention deficit disorder.

In 2006 he was banned again after testosterone 'or its precursors' were found during tests. Gatlin issued a statement saying, 'I cannot account for these results, because I have never knowingly used any banned substance or authorised anyone to administer such a substance to me.' Gatlin avoided lifetime exclusion by accepting an eight-year ban, although this was later halved, due to his cooperation with anti-doping authorities.

His coach Trevor Graham claimed that testosterone got into the athlete's system through a massage therapist rubbing cream into his legs, although the therapist denied this.

Gatlin returned to sprinting in 2010 and in the 2012 London Olympics won bronze in the 100m behind Usain Bolt and Yohan Blake. Gatlin went on to beat Bolt the following year.

SILIC BANNED

Croatian tennis player Marin Čilić was given a nine-month ban in 2013 following a positive test for nikethamide, a prohibited stimulant which assists respiration. He claimed that the test result was due to his taking of glucose tablets. While playing at the Monte Carlo Masters he had run out of the brand he normally took and his mother had gone to a local pharmacy to buy some more. These were the French versions which had different ingredients. His ban was later reduced to four months on appeal to the Court of Arbitration of Sport.

TROICKI SITUATION

At the same tournament that saw Čilić's mother purchasing troublesome glucose tablets, Viktor Troicki missed giving blood as part of a drugs test. He had asked to be excused the test as he was feeling dizzy and unwell. The Serb also claimed he had a phobia of needles, which he had inherited from his father. He was able to provide a urine sample but thought the official had allowed him to postpone the test. He took it the next day (it was negative) but he received official notification that he had been marked as missing a test. Troicki was initially given an 18-month ban, which was then reduced to 12 months. His fellow professionals offered differing views, with Andy Murray calling him (and Čilić) 'unprofessional', but fellow Serb Novak Djokovic called it a 'total injustice'.

THE BUTLER DID IT

Godolphin is a stable for thoroughbred racehorses owned by Sheikh Mohammed bin Rashid Al Maktoum, the ruler of Dubai. It is based in Newmarket. In April 2013 it was revealed that the stable had been doping horses over a number of years.

A visit by the British Horseracing Authority (BHA) found that 11 horses had been given anabolic steroids, including the unbeaten filly Certify. Trainer Mahmood Al Zarooni owned up to the doping, calling it a 'catastrophic mistake'. He was banned for eight years.

While this scandal was being digested, another Newmarket trainer, Gerald Butler, admitted in a newspaper interview that he had also given his horses steroids. He claimed that the use of these substances had been approved by a vet. Butler owned up to injecting some of the horses himself with Rexogin, a steroid used by humans and which is ten times stronger than the veterinary product Sungate. He was banned from racing for five years. The disciplinary panel called his actions 'an appalling breach of his duty to look after the interests of the horses in his care and amounted to conduct that was seriously prejudicial to the integrity, proper conduct and good reputation of horse racing in Great Britain'.

The BHA investigation found that other trainers had also used Sungate, but took no further action, despite it being banned for racehorses.

TYSON KNOCKOUT

Athlete Tyson Gay is the world's second fastest man, with a 100m time of 9.69 seconds, just behind Usain Bolt's world record of 9.58 seconds. In 2012 Gay won silver as part of the USA team in the 4×100m relay in the London Olympics but a year later it was announced he had failed a drugs test, testing positive for a banned substance at the US championships in June, where he had won both the 100m and 200m events. An out-of-competition test in May was also found to be positive. The substance was later revealed to be the hormone DHEA.

When his test results were made public, Gay said: 'I don't have a sabotage story... I basically put my trust in someone and was let down.' Gay's positive test result came as a result of creams and supplements given to him by a chiropractor and anti-ageing specialist called Clayton Gibson III. Gay had expressed concern when he first saw the creams, as they had labels saying 'testosterone/DHEA crème'. Gibson had told Gay that despite the labels, they were 100 per cent natural and that no one who had used them had ever tested positive. Despite both being banned substances, Gay began using them in July 2012.

Due to his cooperation with the US anti-doping authorities, Gay was given a reduced ban of one year. His results from July 2012 onwards were wiped. Included in this was the 4×100m at the Olympics. Gay's teammates also lost their medals as a result of Gay's test. Justin Gatlin, who was no stranger to drugs bans, said, 'I honestly don't mind giving it back if it wasn't won fairly.'

Not everyone was as forgiving as Gatlin. Following Gay's return to athletics after his ban was over, Usain Bolt said, 'It's the stupidest thing I've ever heard. The message should be: "If you cheat you're going to be kicked out of the sport."'

Gay's coach Jon Drummond, who had introduced the athlete to Gibson, was issued with an eight-year ban for possession, trafficking and administration of a banned substance. Drummond was a former Olympic gold medallist in the 4×100m relay and in the 2012 Olympics was coach of the US team. He had been involved in another controversy, during the 2003 World Championships. In a quarter-final for the 100m he was disqualified for false starts but refused to leave, laying down on the track and ignoring the instructions of the officials.

JUST SAY MO

No one who took an interest in the London Olympics of 2012 will ever forget 'Super Saturday' on 4 August, when British athletes won six golds, with three golds in the same evening session: Jessica Ennis in the heptathlon, Greg Rutherford in the long jump and in the 10,000m – Mo Farah, who entered popular consciousness by making the sign of the letter 'M' above his head in what became known as the 'Mobot'. Farah was the first Briton to win an Olympic 10,000m and a week later he won a second Olympic gold in the 5,000m.

In 2011 he moved to America to work with Alberto Salazar, who had set up his Oregon Project, sponsored by sportswear giant Nike, to improve distance-running athletes. Before becoming America's most prominent running coach, Salazar was a successful distance athlete himself, winning three consecutive New York marathons.

At the 10,000m medal ceremony in London in 2012, Farah shared a podium with American runner Galen Rupp, a long-time member of the Oregon Project and a training partner of his.

In June 2015 the BBC and the US investigative team ProPublica alleged that Salazar was advocating steroid use. He was reported to be telling his athletes to take prescription drugs that they had no medical need for. By doing this, athletes would be able to secure TUEs (therapeutic use exemptions) for drugs that would normally be banned, such as asthma inhalers.

Farah was not implicated in the reports but the closeness of these allegations to his training set-up caused him considerable embarrassment. He issued a statement that he had not taken any performance-enhancing drugs and countered a story in the *Daily Mail* in June 2015 alleging he'd missed two drugs tests. He explained that one in February 2011 was missed as he had been sleeping when testing officials arrived at his house. Had Farah missed another test he could have been banned from competing in the Olympics in 2012.

THEY THINK IT'S SHARAPOVA

I made a huge mistake.

Maria Sharapova, 7 March 2016

In March 2016, Russian tennis player Maria Sharapova admitted she had tested positive for a banned substance in the Australian Open, held the previous month. The five-time Grand Slam winner had taken the drug Mildronate (also known as meldonium) for ten years, but it had been placed on the banned substance list in January 2016.

Sharapova explained that she had been prescribed the drug, which helps the blood flow, to deal with an irregular heartbeat and also early signs of diabetes. It was banned because it also offers athletes enhanced performance.

She was suspended from tennis and also suffered financially as Nike suspended its endorsement contract with her, and watchmaker TAG Heuer stopped negotiations for a new deal. Sharapova said, 'I have let my fans down. I've let down the sport that I have been playing since the age of four that I love so deeply. I know that with this I face consequences and I don't want to end my career this way.' In June 2016 she was issued with a two-year ban.

PRO BONAR

In April 2016 *The Sunday Times* printed allegations that a former GP had given banned substances to 150 elite sportsmen and women.

Dr Mark Bonar was secretly filmed saying boxers, Tour de France cyclists, Premier League footballers and tennis players had been given EPO, steroids and HGH.

Premier League clubs Arsenal, Chelsea and Leicester, which had been named in the story, issued strong denials. Leicester, who were top of the league at the time, said: 'Leicester City Football Club is extremely disappointed that the *Sunday Times* has published unsubstantiated allegations referring to players from clubs including Leicester City when, on its own admission, it has insufficient evidence to support the claims.'

In the wake of the scandal, questions were asked about the UK Anti-Doping (UKAD) authority as it was revealed that it had been told about potential issues with Bonar in 2014. The allegations had not been taken further by UKAD or any other body. The UK government ordered an investigation into the allegations soon after they were published.

RECREATIONAL DRUGS

As well as drugs taken to improve performance, sportsmen and women have been known to take other types of substance. This does not always play well with their sport's governing bodies...

KEY SCANDAL: IN HOT WATER

American swimmer Michael Phelps has won 22 Olympic medals – 18 of them gold. He won every one of the eight events he entered at the Beijing games in 2008 – an unprecedented feat. But the reputation of the most decorated Olympian was affected in 2009 when the British tabloid *News of the World* printed a picture of him smoking from a bong. He admitted that the photograph was authentic and was subsequently banned from swimming for three months. It was a drug of a different kind that had got the young American in trouble in 2004 when, aged 19, he had been convicted of drink-driving in Maryland. In 2014 he was found guilty of drink-driving and speeding.

'E's ARE NOT GOOD

In 1999 England rugby captain Lawrence Dallaglio was embroiled in a scandal when a newspaper alleged he had both used and sold drugs before he played rugby. He was also reported to have celebrated the British and Irish Lions' victory in South Africa in 1997 by taking ecstasy and cocaine.

The England captain strenuously denied the story and said it was a set-up. His mother backed him, saying, 'If my son took drugs, then I would know about it. He has always been a level-headed boy.'

The *News of the World* stood by their story, with editor Phil Hall saying, 'We are amazed at his denial.' Dallaglio resigned the captaincy the day after the story broke, following a meeting with the Rugby Football Union. After an investigation was carried out he was fined £15,000 for bringing the game into disrepute. Dallaglio later regained the captaincy.

CAUGHT AND BANNED

Spectators can enjoy cricket with a relaxing beer or cup of tea, as the overs are played out over several days. It is also a sport where some of the players are not averse to relaxing with something a bit stronger and a bit more illegal:

- England's tour of New Zealand in 1983–4 was marred by allegations of drug-taking which were investigated by the New Zealand police but resulted in no further action. One of the players on the tour was Ian Botham, who in 1986 was suspended for two months for admitting in a newspaper article to taking cannabis. Botham had been fined £100 for possession of cannabis in 1985.

- West Indian wicketkeeper David Murray admitted to smoking cannabis since he was a young teenager. He also confessed to having taken cocaine. Murray was unable to secure a long-term place in the West Indies side of the

1980s and was banned after going on a rebel tour of South Africa. Murray admitted to smoking cannabis before and after games to help his concentration.

- In 1993 four Pakistani players, Waqar Younis, Aqib Javed, Mushtaq Ahmed and Wasim Akram, were arrested on charges of possessing cannabis on a beach in Grenada. They spent the night in the cells but charges were dropped.

- Following a poor tour of South Africa in 1993–4, New Zealand players Stephen Fleming, Dion Nash and Matthew Hart were all issued bans after being caught smoking cannabis at a barbecue. Echoing comments once made by US President Bill Clinton, Nash claimed he had 'simulated' rather than smoked.

- Fast bowler Ed Giddins was given an 18-month ban for taking cocaine in 1996. He was also sacked by his county team Sussex. In 2004 Giddins was fined £5,000 and banned for five years for betting on his team Surrey to lose a match in August 2002.

- Paul Smith of Warwickshire admitted taking cannabis, speed and cocaine in 1997. He was banned for two years.

- England spin bowler Phil Tufnell was alleged to have smoked cannabis in a restaurant's disabled toilet while on tour in New Zealand in 1996–7. He was cleared, but after failing to appear for a random drugs test in 1997 he was fined £1,000 and given an 18-month suspended ban.

- Five South African players were fined 10,000 rand for smoking cannabis while on tour in the West Indies in

2001. Herschelle Gibbs, Roger Telemachus, Andre Nel, Paul Adams, Justin Kemp and team physiotherapist Craig Smith were celebrating a Test series victory when they were reported by another player for smoking the drug in their hotel rooms.

- In 2005 the 35-year-old Keith Piper of Warwickshire was given a four-month ban after a drugs test came back positive for cannabis.

- In 2005 ex-England all-rounder Dermot Reeve confessed to a cocaine addiction and as a result lost his job as a television commentator. He also admitted to smoking cannabis while captain of Warwickshire.

ON THE LINE

I have tested positive, but I have never taken drugs and I feel 100 per cent innocent.

Martina Hingis, November 2007

Swiss tennis player Martina Hingis has won five Grand Slam singles tournaments as well as 12 women's doubles and four mixed titles. Named after Martina Navratilova, she became the youngest Grand Slam winner in 1996 when she won the women's doubles championship at Wimbledon alongside Helena Suková. Hingis was 15 years and 9 months old. Hingis's 'youngest ever' achievements continued when she became the youngest Grand Slam singles champion at the Australian Open in 1997, aged 16, and the youngest world number one later that year.

In November 2007 the Swiss player shocked the tennis world when she announced she had tested positive for cocaine, the test being carried out during Wimbledon. She stated she was terrified of taking drugs. Hingis announced her retirement, saying that although she felt there were inconsistencies with the test and its processing, she did not have the will to take on the anti-doping authorities. She also cited her age and health problems as reasons not to continue. In 2008 she was banned from tennis for two years but returned to the sport in 2013 and won the women's doubles title at Wimbledon in 2015, partnering Sania Mirza. The pair went on to success in the US Open and then in 2016 won the Australian Open.

ANOTHER FINE METH

Andre Agassi was a flamboyant baseliner, who secured eight Grand Slam tournaments in a 21-year professional tennis career. He retired in 2006 and three years later published his autobiography. In it he revealed he had failed a drugs test in 1997. The substance found was crystal meth, the crystalline form of the highly addictive stimulant methamphetamine. Agassi explained in a letter to the ATP that he had taken the drug by accident, which had been put in a soft drink, spiked by his assistant. The ATP accepted this, but in his book he revealed he had lied and had taken it willingly. He said the drug gave him 'a tidal wave of euphoria that sweeps away every negative thought in my head'.

Agassi had been suffering a slump in his career at this point – he was ranked 141 in the world – but he embarked on a fitness programme and played his way back to the top levels of the game. In 1997 he married Hollywood actress Brooke

Shields but they divorced two years later. She later blamed his drug addiction as one of the reasons behind their break-up. Agassi remarried in 2001 to 22-time Grand Slam winner Steffi Graf.

In his autobiography, Agassi also wrote that he did not like the game in which he had made his name and fortune. He said, 'I play tennis for a living, even though I hate tennis with a dark and secret passion, and always have.'

BLOWN A GASQUET

French tennis player Richard Gasquet was banned for 12 months in 2009 when a drugs test found cocaine in his system. His ban was reduced to two and a half months by a tribunal that investigated the circumstances following his positive test in Miami in March that year. Gasquet had withdrawn with a shoulder injury from the Miami Masters tournament before even hitting a ball, and had gone on a night out. During the evening he spent time in a nightclub where he hit it off with a woman – known in the subsequent inquiry as 'Pamela' – and the Frenchman's French-kissing with Pamela was accepted as the reason the drug entered his system.

UNSPORTING BEHAVIOUR

Unsporting behaviour is that which stays on the correct side of the relevant laws but strays into territory that might be deemed suspect on ethical grounds. Some of sport's greatest names have had their reputations affected by allegations that their behaviour was not what some thought it should be.

KEY SCANDAL: BECKS IS OFF

The footballing rivalry between England and Argentina, which had begun in 1966, continued into the 1998 World Cup in France when they met in the second round on 30 June in Saint-Étienne. Shortly after the half-time break and with the scores level at 2–2, England midfielder David Beckham was fouled from behind by Diego Simeone. Beckham fell to the ground with the Argentinian falling on top. Simeone pushed up using his hand on Beckham's back and then Beckham, still lying on the ground, flicked his leg up and caught his opponent on the leg. The Argentinian fell backwards.

Beckham received a straight red card by Danish referee Kim Milton Nielsen, becoming only the second England player to be sent off during a World Cup. (Ray Wilkins had been ordered off in 1986's tournament.)

The match ended 2–2 after extra time. England had a goal chalked off when the referee ruled striker Alan Shearer had fouled the Argentinian goalkeeper before Sol Campbell headed in. The match went to penalties. Following on from their lack of success in the 1996 European Championships when they'd lost out to Germany in the semi-finals, England lost the shoot-out 4–3, with Paul Ince and David Batty failing to score.

Despite the missed penalties and Shearer's foul, it was Beckham who was the focus of public criticism. The *Daily Mirror* headline the next day read '10 Heroic Lions, One Stupid Boy'. A church in Nottingham put up a sign saying 'God Forgives Even David Beckham'. An effigy of him in his England number 7 shirt was hung outside a London pub and he received death threats. At the first game of the new domestic season, the Manchester United player had to be given a police escort.

In 2002 Simeone admitted he had made the most of the incident, saying, 'If you don't take advantage of a chance that comes your way you are lost.'

That year England met Argentina for the fourth time in the World Cup. The match was won 1–0, with England's goal coming from a penalty scored by David Beckham. He had also scored the goal that ensured England's qualification for the tournament with a magnificent 30-yard, last-minute free kick against Greece.

Beckham said of the events of 1998, 'I knew that I had made a mistake and deserved to be sent off, but nothing could have prepared me for what happened.'

AMAZING GRACE

Victorian W. G. Grace is commonly regarded as one of the greatest cricketers to have played the game. He was easily recognisable, with his large beard and large build, and is credited with popularising cricket as a national game. The list of his achievements is as long as his 44-season career as a cricketer:

- He scored over 54,000 runs in first-class matches.

- He took over 2,800 wickets as a bowler.

- His record innings of 344 (from 1876) stood for 19 years.

- He came to public attention when, as a 15 year old, he scored 170 for South Wales.

- In 1895, aged 47, he scored 1,000 runs before the end of May, reaching an unprecedented 100 three-figure scores.

- He once declared while still at the crease on a score of 93 because it was the only figure from 0 to 100 he hadn't achieved.

- Taking a turn as wicketkeeper against Australia in 1884, he became the only one to make a catch off the first ball bowled to him.

- In 1886 against Oxford he hit a century and took all ten opposing wickets – a feat only ever repeated by one other player in a first-class match.

- He played in 1,478 first-class innings.

Grace made his first-class debut on 22 June 1865 when he took the field for Gentlemen of the South against the Players of the South. Grace was a Gentleman, an amateur, while the Players were the professionals. It was in this area that Grace pushed the boundaries into what was known as 'shamateurism', as he earned more than the professional Players. He was very much aware of his crowd-pulling place in the game and on his first tour of Australia in 1873–4 he insisted on a fee of £1,500, the modern equivalent of £100,000. On his second tour in 1891–2 a fifth of the money given to the England team for the expense of travelling and staying in Australia went to Grace. Those in the game were not unaware of the financial benefits he accrued and he was not always regarded with the fondness of those who paid to watch him.

Grace was ultra-competitive in nature and was known for what could be termed gamesmanship. In one innings, when the ball stuck in his shirt after being played by him he continued to make runs, insisting that if he touched the ball he'd put himself out. On another occasion, when bowled by fast bowler Charles Kortright he was slow to leave the crease. Kortright called to him, 'Surely not going, doctor? One of the stumps is still standing!'

It was this competitive streak that saw him create a scandal in 1878. Batsman Billy Midwinter, who was born in Gloucestershire, emigrated to Australia and played against England in 1877. He moved back to England the same year to play for Grace's Gloucestershire, becoming their first professional player.

In 1878 Australia were touring England and Midwinter was selected to play for his adopted antipodean country.

It is reputed that Midwinter had an agreement with Grace that he would play for his country when required. On 20 June, Midwinter was about to play for Australia against Middlesex at Lord's, on the same day Gloucestershire had a county match against Surrey at the Oval. When he heard that his player was not going to turn out for his county employer, Grace raced over to Lord's and 'convinced' Midwinter, who was padded up ready to bat, to change his mind. Some reports have him being bundled into a cab while still in his playing gear.

The Australians made pursuit but, despite an angry exchange of views, Grace was not to be persuaded and Midwinter duly played for his county. Grace's 'kidnapping' didn't work, as his county lost their first match for two years. Midwinter played in both innings, scoring 4 and 0. The Australian touring party were not impressed and threatened to abandon plans to play against Gloucestershire. Grace had to apologise for the 'unparliamentary language' he had used when calling the Australians 'a lot of sneaks' before the Australians agreed to play as scheduled.

Grace played his last first-class game in 1908 and died on 23 October 1915, aged 67. It was said his demise was accelerated by him waving his fist in defiance at Zeppelins as they attacked London as part of the German aerial offensive against the capital.

ROCK THE BODY

There are two teams out there; one is trying to play cricket and the other is not.

Bill Woodfull, captain of Australia

During the 1932–3 Ashes tour of Australia, the cricket world was rocked by a Test match series like no other – one that is still discussed to this day.

The great Australian player of this age – and of any age – was Don Bradman. His batting prowess is shown in his scores when defeating England in the Ashes Tests of 1930. He made 974 runs, an average of 139. The following year, against South Africa, his average was 201. He was a master of the batting arts and to stop him on the harder Australian pitches would require something special.

The English captain was the Scottish-sounding Douglas Robert Jardine. That's because he was Scottish, born to Scots parents in 1900. His ruthlessness in wanting victory was highlighted when he was reported to have said, 'I've not travelled six thousand miles to make friends. I'm here to win the Ashes.'

England did not want to face a whitewash in the Ashes tour and so devised a method to counter Bradman's skill at the crease. It was what the Australians called 'bodyline bowling' and their opponents England called 'fast leg theory'. It was where the ball was bowled towards the batsman's body, on the line of the leg stump, in the hope of causing deflections or defensive strokes that could be caught by fielders who were placed close in, in a ring on the leg side, in a 'leg trap'. Players' protective equipment at the time was the bare minimum and this type of bowling would be seen as intimidatory. Jardine had noticed through watching film footage of a previous Test match that Bradman appeared to be afraid of short-pitched balls that hit him directly. The tactics weren't new and such a style of bowling and fielding had been done before, but not at the intensity that would now be carried out. England had in Harold Larwood a fast bowler of great accuracy and speed. Along with Bill Voce, he was tasked with delivering victory.

In the first test, Bradman was ill and played no part. England won by ten wickets. In the second, Bradman was bowled out first ball but Australia went on to win the match.

It was the third test, at Adelaide, that would be remembered, two balls in particular, both bowled by Larwood. One hit the Australian captain Bill Woodfull in the chest, just above his heart as he ducked to avoid a short delivery. England captain Jardine was heard to say to his bowler Larwood, 'Well bowled, Harold.' The other ball hit Bert Oldfield in the head, fracturing his skull, as he ducked to avoid the ball. The crowd were not best pleased with this, but to lay the blame at the bodyline door would be wrong, as both balls were not of the bodyline type. However, this was not appreciated by the crowd. There was rising outrage at the English tactics.

At the end of the fourth day's play the Australian cricket authority sent this message to the MCC (Marylebone Cricket Club – cricket's governing body at the time):

Bodyline bowling has assumed such proportions as to menace the best interests of the game, making protection of the body by the batsmen the main consideration. This is causing intensely bitter feeling between the players as well as injury. In our opinion it is unsportsmanlike. Unless stopped at once it is likely to upset the friendly relations existing between Australia and England.

An international crisis developed, until the Australian allegation of unsporting behaviour was withdrawn. The Ashes were retained by England 4–1 but the rules were eventually changed to make bodyline bowling impossible.

RATTIN CARPETED

The rivalry between Argentina and England sparked to life in the football World Cup held in England in 1966. Despite the sporting links between the nations – it was British nationals who had introduced the game to the country – these were quickly forgotten when scandal hit.

England had reached the quarter-finals, where they met Argentina. In the thirty-fifth minute of a scrappy and unruly game the Argentinian captain Antonio Rattin was sent off for reasons that weren't explained clearly. It was suggested his style of badgering the referee became too much for the West German whistler Rudolf Kreitlein, who snapped and sent him off. Rattin had been booked previously for a tackle on Bobby Charlton. (After the game, Kreitlein was quoted saying, 'I do not speak Spanish but the look on his face was enough.')

Ten minutes of disruption ensued as Rattin – wearing the number 10, which would be worn by another Argentinian who would appear in football scandals – refused to leave the field. Argentinian players surrounded the referee. Rattin said it took so long to deal with the incident because he was seeking an interpreter. Once off the pitch he sat down at one point on the red carpet reserved for VIPs.

The game was decided by a solitary goal, scored by Geoff Hurst in the seventy-eighth minute – and to add to the bad feeling, the Argentinians felt it was offside. England coach Alf Ramsey ordered his team not to swap jerseys at the end of the game and called the opponents 'animals'.

Afterwards, the FIFA disciplinary committee issued their penalties:

- Argentina's football association was fined the maximum amount allowed: 1,000 Swiss francs (equivalent to £85).

- Rattin was suspended for four Argentina games.

- Roberto Ferreiro (who was found to have attacked the referee) was suspended for three international matches.

- Ermindo Onega (who was found to have spat at the game's official observer) was suspended for three international matches.

It was also suggested that Argentina could be barred from taking part in the 1970 World Cup unless they promised to behave. The Argentinian football association president said, 'I do not approve of the conduct of our players and officials but they were provoked by the referee. He was absolutely biased in favour of England.' The Argentina players were given a heroes' welcome on their return home, while the British ambassador was advised to remain in his embassy for a few days until it all died down. To Argentinians, the game became known as 'el robo del siglo' – the theft of the century.

UNDERARM AND UNDERHAND

One of the worst things I have ever seen done
on a cricket field.

Richie Benaud, Australian cricket player and commentator

This incident took place in a match between the two rival cricketing countries of Australia and New Zealand. The one-day World Series Cup final was tied after two matches. The third match out of the five-match series was held at Melbourne Cricket Ground on 1 February 1981.

Australia batted first and reached 235. New Zealand chased this total and, with one over left and four wickets remaining, were 15 runs short of a victory, or 14 for a draw.

Trevor Chappell was the Australian bowler for this infamous last over:

1st ball	A four from Hadlee.
2nd ball	Hadlee bowled out. Ian Smith comes on. New Zealand need 11 to win from 4 balls remaining.
3rd ball	Smith hits, 2 runs gained.
4th ball	Another 2 runs.
5th ball	Smith bowled out.
6th ball	Brian McKechnie replaces Smith. New Zealand can tie the game if they hit a 6.

What then took place was later described by the New Zealand prime minister Robert Muldoon as 'the most disgusting incident I can recall in the history of cricket'.

Under instruction from Australian captain Greg Chappell, his brother Trevor bowled underarm, trundling the ball towards McKechnie. Trevor Chappell later admitted he knew it wasn't in the spirit of the game but seemed a good idea at the time.

Australia had won. Walking off the pitch, McKechnie threw his bat down in disgust. Australia won the next match by six wickets and so the series. The following year, when Australia visited New Zealand, the home fans rolled carpet bowls on to the pitch.

THE UMPIRE STRIKES BACK

*You are a f***ing cheat.*

Shakoor Rana, 8 December 1987

Mike Gatting was a cricketer for whom the word pugnacious may have been invented. As well as a rugged competitor, he was a gifted batsman, adept at dealing with spin bowlers. In a One Day International against the West Indies in 1986, a bouncer by Malcolm Marshall smashed into Gatting's nose with so much force that fragments of bone were found stuck into the ball. He returned to play in the final Test match.

Gatting was given the captainship of England in 1986 and led the side to an unexpected Ashes win in Australia in 1986–7 and was in charge when England went to tour Pakistan in November and December 1987. In the second Test at Faisalabad he was accused by Pakistani umpire Shakoor Rana of having a fielder move position while one of his bowlers was in the act of bowling. Gatting countered that his signal to the fielder, David Capel, was to tell him to stop moving. The signal was out of the batsman's sight.

It became a confrontation that quickly blew up and led to Rana calling Gatting a cheat. Angry words were exchanged and fingers were pointed by both parties. There was no play the following day. A stand-off about who should apologise to whom meant it dragged on until the fourth day, when Gatting gave a handwritten apology to Rana.

The incident led to neutral umpires being used. English players had not been impressed by Rana wearing a Pakistan jumper under his umpire's jacket.

Gatting lost the captaincy the following year. A tabloid had printed a story that he had had sex with a woman in his hotel one night in the middle of a Test match at Trent Bridge. Both Gatting and the woman denied having sex but both admitted he had invited the woman to his room – but as part of a party with other cricketers and hotel staff, who never turned up. Another factor in him losing the captaincy was the publication of his autobiography, *Leading from the Front*, which hadn't had the approval of the Test and County Cricket Board.

TUMBA OUT

In September 1991, Swedish golfer Johan Tumba was attempting to enter the PGA Qualifying School. At the end of his round at the Quiet Waters golf club in Essex he signed his scorecard with a round of 72. The problem was he had actually shot a 74. His playing partner Ian Roper told the officials, who issued him with a ten-year ban.

SCHU OFF #1

Michael Schumacher is one of motor racing's great champions. He was the consummate professional driver, whose qualities were clear from the start. In his very first Formula One race he qualified seventh at Spa in Belgium. Racing for Benetton the next year, he won his first race, also at Spa. His career was to see an unprecedented series of records:

- He won the F1 championship seven times.

- He came first in 91 races.

- He achieved 98 pole positions.

- He was on the podium for every race in the 2002 season – the only driver ever to have achieved such a feat.

But among Schumacher's great successes there were moments of controversy. By the last race of the 1994 season, the Australian Grand Prix at Adelaide, Schumacher was one point ahead of British rival Damon Hill. On lap 36, Hill made an attempt to overtake but Schumacher's car came across and collided, his own car lifting up and bouncing across and off the track. Hill's car was damaged and he was forced to retire. The German had won his first world championship.

SCHU OFF #2

Schumacher won the drivers' championship in 1995, but in 1996 Damon Hill took the title, emulating the success of his father Graham. The 1997 championship drew to a climax in a similar way to that of 1994, but instead of Hill, Schumacher was one point ahead of Canadian driver Jacques Villeneuve. (Villeneuve was, like Hill, the son of a famous F1 driver – Gilles, who was killed in an accident in 1982.) Schumacher would win his third world championship if he finished in front of Villeneuve at the European Grand Prix in Spain.

Villeneuve started the race in pole position but Schumacher overtook him straight away and continued in the lead through 47 laps. In the forty-eighth lap, the pursuing Villeneuve saw his opportunity and, coming into the Dry Sack corner, made to overtake. Schumacher then cut across, his Ferrari's right front wheel hitting the left-side radiator of Villeneuve's Williams. The German's car went off the track and was unable to continue. Villeneuve carried on with his damaged car and finished third, gaining enough points to claim the title, which would be his sole F1 championship.

The sport's governing body, the Fédération Internationale de l'Automobile (FIA) later disqualified Schumacher from the championship. Max Mosley, the FIA's president said, 'Although the actions were deliberate, they were not premeditated.' Schumacher admitted an error of judgement. The German said in 2006, 'If there were a situation in my career which I could undo, it would be this.'

SCHU OFF #3

Michael Schumacher had won five successive drivers' championships between 2000 and 2004. In his last victorious season, he won 13 of the 18 races. The 2005 season saw him finish third. In the 2006 season he once again courted controversy, owing to his actions at Monaco, the most famous of all the Grand Prix circuits. During qualifying, Schumacher had clinched pole position, but while still on the track he stopped his car at the Rascasse corner. By doing so he prevented his nearest rival, Fernando Alonso, from setting a faster time and taking pole from him. He claimed it was an error but the stewards thought otherwise and Schumacher was relegated to the back of the grid. Among the many drivers and ex-drivers who thought it deliberate, 1982 champion Keke Rosberg said, 'It was the cheapest, dirtiest thing I have ever seen in F1. He should leave F1 and go home.' In the race, Schumacher's superb driving ability was shown as he reached fifth position.

Schumacher retired at the end of the season but returned in 2010 for a spell with Mercedes, before retiring for good two years later. In December 2013, he suffered a severe head injury while skiing at Meribel in the French Alps. He entered a coma and only left hospital in September the following year, but he is understood to be paralysed and unable to speak.

RED CARPET TREATMENT

When England's rugby team came to Dublin's Lansdowne Road in 2003, a crucial match lay ahead. Either Ireland or England could win the Grand Slam and the Six Nations championship. Ireland were chasing their first Grand Slam in 55 years, while England's last one was more recent, in 1995.

The battle began before a ball had even been kicked or carried: when England captain Martin Johnson led his team out, he made his players line up in front of the red carpet – in the area where the home side would normally stand. Despite being invited to move along, Johnson refused, thus forcing the Irish team to line up on the grass. This meant that the VIP being presented to the teams – Ireland's president Mary McAleese –

had to shake hands while walking across the turf rather than the red carpet rolled out for this purpose.

The gamesmanship might have played a part as England ran out 42–6 winners and won the Grand Slam. Johnson later claimed he had no intention of causing any embarrassment and would have moved had the match referee asked.

THE RULE MONTY

During the Indonesian Open in 2005, Scots golfer Colin Montgomerie was feeling the pressure. In the second round, on the fourteenth hole, 'Monty' put his ball into a bunker. It left him with a difficult stance to play the next shot, with one leg in the bunker and the other out. As he considered his options, lightning interrupted play and the golfers went off the course. Before he left, Montgomerie failed to mark the position of the ball. When he returned the next day his ball was gone. He put down a new ball and resumed his round – he went on to win the tournament. TV evidence later showed that the ball was about a foot away from where it had been, thus giving him an easier stance. Monty faced no action but he did give away his prize money to charity. The officials accepted it was unintentional and no action was taken against the Scot. However, some within the game felt otherwise and Montgomerie was criticised by some fellow professionals, such as Sandy Lyle.

FEELING PIQUET

Nelson Piquet was a three-time winner of the F1 drivers' championship. His son Nelson Junior was born in 1985 and followed his father behind the wheel. Nelson Junior was a talented young driver and got his chance with a F1 team in 2007 when he joined Renault. The next year he raced alongside two-time world champion Fernando Alonso. He had a poor start but ended the season having been on the podium at the German Grand Prix, where he finished second to Lewis Hamilton.

In 2009 he was retained by Renault, but a poor season in which he collected no points saw him sacked from the team in July. Not long after he left Renault, Piquet told the FIA he had deliberately crashed in the previous year's Singapore Grand Prix in order to assist his teammate Alonso – who went on to win the race. Piquet gave evidence to the FIA that he was asked to crash his car by team boss Flavio Briatore and engineer Pat Symonds. Renault initially denied the allegations but later accepted they were true. Both Briatore and Symonds left the team.

The race involving 'Crashgate' had seen Alonso begin fifteenth and Piquet behind him in sixteenth. Alonso was first to pit, going in on the twelfth lap. While on his fourteenth lap, Piquet crashed into a wall. The safety car came out while the wreckage was cleared off the track. The cars in front of Alonso then had to pit and he was able to move up the field to claim victory.

Piquet was unable to secure another drive in Formula One but went on to drive in NASCAR. Briatore and Symonds received bans from the sport.

GIMME GIMME SHOCK TREATMENT

I have never seen anything like it in my career.

Juli Inkster, USA team captain

The Solheim Cup is a biennial tournament played between teams of professional female golfers from the USA and Europe. It is not an event known for scandal, but that was to change in 2015, at St Leon-Rot in Germany.

In the four-ball matches, Norwegian Suzann Pettersen and Britain's Charley Hull were playing America's Brittany Lincicome and Alison Lee. Their game was carried over to the Sunday morning following suspension of play the previous evening due to bad light.

The match was all square after 16 holes. On the seventeenth green, Lee had a birdie putt from 12 feet. Her putt missed, and the ball rolled past the hole by about 16 inches.

Europe's Hull started to walk to the next tee, indicating the putt was a 'gimme' – conceded without the opposing player having to putt. Lee lifted her ball. However, Pettersen said she had to putt. Because the American had lifted the ball, the match officials had to award the hole to the Europeans. The Europeans won the eighteenth hole and the match ended as a 2–0 victory for them.

The Americans were outraged at what took place on the seventeenth hole and team captain Juli Inkster said, 'It's just not right. You just don't do that to your peers. It's disrespectful.' Both Lee and her opponent Hull were seen in tears. Pettersen later apologised, writing on social media: 'I was trying my hardest for my team and put the single match and the point that could be earned ahead of sportsmanship and the game of golf itself! I feel like I let my team down and I am sorry.'

At the end of the four-balls the USA were 10–6 down, but the incident served as motivation and they fought back to win the Cup 14½ to 13½.

BALL-TAMPERING

In ball sports, with so much resting on the flight of the ball, it is not surprising that attempts are made to alter it to gain an advantage. In cricket, for example, tampering can produce 'reverse swing' where the ball moves more than expected and causes problems for the batsman. Bowlers who wish to achieve this will rough up one side of the ball, or polish up the other. It is not illegal to polish the ball – the red marks on the front of bowlers' trousers show where they have been doing this – but it is illegal to go further. Where the line is drawn is often open to interpretation.

KEY SCANDAL: DEFLATEGATE

Professional American football is organised by the National Football League (NFL). Two conferences play as part of this: the American Football Conference (AFC) and the National Football Conference (NFC). At the end of the season a series of play-offs culminate in the Super Bowl, which features the two winners of the AFC and the NFC's Championship Games.

On 18 January 2015, at the Gillette Stadium, Massachusetts, the New England Patriots faced the Indianapolis Colts in the AFC Championship Game. During the game, officials were notified that some of the footballs being used were below regulation pressure. There is an advantage to an attacking team in having softer footballs as they are easier to handle. In American football, teams are allowed to provide their players with their own footballs.

Despite the issue, the game continued and the result was a 45–7 win for the Patriots. They were now going to the Super Bowl.

An inquiry by the NFL was carried out. The 243-page Wells Report, prepared by attorney Theodore 'Ted' Wells, was issued in May 2015. It stated:

> ***Based on the evidence developed in connection with the investigation and summarised in this Report, we have concluded that it is more probable than not that New England Patriots personnel participated in violations of the NFL Playing Rules and were involved in a deliberate attempt to circumvent those rules.***

The report also stated that it was 'more probable than not' that Patriots' quarterback Tom Brady was 'at least generally aware' that air was released from the footballs. Brady was suspended for four games but his suspension was overturned by a judge. Two of the Patriots' backroom staff, John Jastremski and Jim McNally, who had been highlighted as probably responsible for the deflation of the footballs, were suspended in May but reinstated in September.

The huge public debate about the issue continued throughout the year. *Rolling Stone* magazine described 'Deflategate' as 'the most absurd scandal in modern sports history', being 'wonderfully stupid and bereft of nobility'.

The Patriots won the Super Bowl, defeating the Seattle Seahawks 28–24.

MADRAS ON THE LINE

John Lever was a left-arm fast-medium bowler who played his club cricket for Essex and internationally for England in 21 Tests and 22 One Day Internationals. Lever made an immediate impact in his first Test against India by taking 7 wickets for 46 runs and 3 for 24 at Delhi in December 1976. However, it wasn't his performance as a bowler that was to be remembered from this tour.

Playing in the hot conditions meant the players were sweating heavily; in the third Test in Madras, Lever and fellow bowler Bob Willis were each given a gauze strip covered in Vaseline by the team's physiotherapist to put on their forehead to stop the sweat getting into their eyes. Sweatbands were not available.

The solution didn't last long as it wasn't very effective, so Lever discarded his. When it was brought to the attention of Indian captain Bishan Bedi by the match's umpire, he accused England of ball-tampering, of applying the Vaseline to the ball. England denied it was deliberate ball-tampering, reasoning that they would have used more subtle methods than a gauze strip stuck on the forehead. Bedi later admitted that Lever was being made a scapegoat as India were under pressure, being 2–0 down in the series.

England went on to win the series 3–1 but Lever was never to achieve the same level of performance again in Test matches.

In 2010 the England captain Tony Greig said, 'I am quite happy to admit right now that it should never have happened, but it did, and there is nothing much we could do about it.'

KHAN-DO SPIRIT

Pakistan's Imran Khan is regarded as one of cricket's great all-rounders. In his career he took 362 Test wickets and scored 3,807 runs in 88 Test matches. He played in England for Sussex.

In a county match against Warwickshire in 1983, Imran Khan recorded 6–6: six wickets taken for just six runs conceded. Warwickshire batsman Chris Old – who was bowled for a duck by Khan – thought something untoward was behind Khan's prowess. He said, 'I saw the ball he'd tampered with and it looked like a dog had chewed it.' The game's umpire Don Oslear also suspected something was up, as the ball was so torn a piece was sticking out so big the ball could be suspended by a thumb and index finger. He was reported to have sent a report to Lord's but nothing further ensued from the incident.

BOTTLING IT

Pakistani batsman Qasim Umar admitted ball-tampering with a bottle top in a Test against England in Karachi in 1984. Pakistan won the match and went on to win the three-match series. Umar claimed his teammates had planned how they would beat England when in Australia a few months previously. He said, 'Schoolboys as young as 12 get to know how to use a bottle top in Pakistan and they've come to think that it's all part of the game.'

PITCH (NOT) PERFECT

Joe Niekro was a Major League Baseball pitcher who played for several teams during his career, but it was while wearing the uniform of the Minnesota Twins in 1987 that he gained notoriety.

During a game against the California Angels, Niekro was asked to empty his pockets by the game's umpire. As he did so, two items fell out and landed on the ground. One was a piece of sandpaper and the other an emery board.

Niekro explained by saying, 'Being a knuckleball pitcher, I sometimes have to file my nails between innings.' Gene Mauch, the manager of the Angels was not convinced and thought that there was no question Niekro had been tampering with the ball saying: 'Nobody ever suspected Joe Niekro. Everybody always *knew* it.'

Niekro was suspended for ten days.

TOP EFFORT

Chris Pringle was a bowler for New Zealand when his country was touring Pakistan in the autumn of 1990. They had lost the first Test and in the second Test, which resulted in another defeat, the New Zealand players noticed the ball was in a ragged state. Batsman Martin Crowe later said, 'We accepted that Pakistan were the better team, but we were not going to accept what they were doing with the ball.'

Along with other bowlers, Pringle started experimenting with how a cricket ball could be altered to give a beneficial effect. In the next Test, he used a cut-up bottle top on the ball. Pakistan, who had got to 35 for 0, were all bowled for 102 in their first innings. Pringle achieved 7–52 – his best ever bowling in a Test match. It didn't affect the overall result as Pakistan won the series 3–0.

SWING BALL

In 1992 Pakistan had won their first Cricket World Cup, defeating favourites England in the final in Melbourne with a display that included Wasim Akram bowling out Allan Lamb and Chris Lewis in successive deliveries. Ian Botham had been bowled out for a duck so England were keen to exact revenge in Pakistan's summer tour of England.

This saw Pakistan's fast bowlers Akram and Waqar Younis enjoying great success with reverse-swing bowling.

After the first Test at Edgbaston was drawn, the second Test at Lord's was won by Pakistan, with Younis bowling 5–91 in the first innings and Akram 4–66. Suitably it was with both players batting together that the final runs were made to win the match.

During the third Test at Old Trafford, Pakistan's bowler Aaqib Javed and captain Javed Miandad had a spat with English umpire Roy Palmer over an incident in which Javed accused Palmer of throwing his jumper at him. Palmer had previously warned him for intimidatory bowling. The bowler was later fined half his match fee.

The fourth Test saw England fight back to win, but in the fifth Test Pakistan won with Akram bowling 6–67 in the first innings and Younis achieving 5–52 in England's second. Pakistan won the Test match series 2–1 amid much speculation by their hosts as to how they had achieved such results, but it was during the one-day series that a full-blown storm would develop.

In the fourth one-day game being played at Lord's the ball was ordered to be changed by umpires Ken Palmer and John Hampshire. Akram and Younis took the new ball and thrashed through England's middle and lower order. After the match the third umpire Don Oslear wanted to disclose the reasons behind the ball change – due to tampering – but the Test and County Cricket Board (TCCB) thought otherwise and so no explanation was given. Mystery and intrigue ensued, as the replaced ball was not produced and was locked away, reportedly in an official's desk drawer. Waqar Younis said, 'I don't care what anyone thinks – the new ball swung more anyway. Every time we win, people start to say those things. We won fair and square.'

Akram and Younis were accused by England player Allan Lamb of ball-tampering and being cheats. His newspaper article in the *Daily Mirror* resulted in a court case with another Pakistan bowler, albeit one who had retired, Sarfraz Nawaz, whom Lamb claimed had showed him how to tamper with the ball. In court Lamb had to admit he'd never seen Nawaz actually carry out any ball-tampering and the case was dropped. Lamb was fined £4,000 by the TCCB, who took a dim view of a player accusing other professionals in public.

WRATH OF KHAN

In September 1981 a County Championship cricket game between Sussex and Hampshire looked to be heading for a draw. In his 1994 authorised biography, Sussex's Imran Khan said, 'The ball was not deviating. I got the twelfth man to bring out a bottle top and it started to move around a lot.' Hampshire were quickly bowled out and Sussex went on to win by nine wickets. In his book he also admitted that in games he had 'occasionally scratched the side of the ball and lifted the seam'. Khan's admission of ball-tampering was met with outrage from the press. Khan did not backtrack, saying it was just part of cricket and he wasn't the only one doing it.

Matters were compounded by an interview in *India Today* when he suggested English players' criticisms were founded on racism and that players like Botham and Lamb did not have the right upbringing or were not of the right class. A court case resulted in 1996, with Botham and Lamb suing Khan for libel. They lost and faced £400,000 in costs. Ian Botham later wrote in his autobiography, 'I felt it was time to set the record straight.'

DIRT IN POCKET

In 1994, during a Test match against South Africa at Lord's, England cricket captain Mike Atherton was spotted on TV cameras taking something out of his pocket and rubbing it onto the cricket ball. The substance turned out to be dirt, which he'd picked up from the ground.

He denied tampering with the ball, and said he was using the dirt to dry his hands, on what was a hot and humid day. Atherton was fined £1,000 by the TCCB for using the dirt and another £1,000 for giving incomplete information to the match referee when asked what he had been doing.

YOUNIS NAILED

Playing against South Africa in the Singer Cup in 2000, Pakistan cricketer Waqar Younis was caught by TV cameras tampering with the ball, by scratching it with his fingernails. He was suspended for one game and lost half his match fee in a fine. Fellow Pakistan player Azhar Mahmood was also fined, losing 30 per cent of his fee. Pakistan's captain Moin Khan was reprimanded for 'allowing the spirit of the game to be impaired'.

DENNESS THE MENACE

In the second Test between South Africa and India in Port Elizabeth in November 2001, match referee Mike Denness ruled that six Indian players be punished:

- Four were cited for excessive appealing: Harbhajan Singh, Virender Sehwag, Shiv Sunder Das, Deep Dasgupta. Sehwag was also accused of dissent.

- India's captain Sourav Ganguly was included for not controlling his players.

- Sachin Tendulkar was alleged to have tampered with the ball.

All these players were fined 75 per cent of their match fees and given suspended one-match bans, except for Sehwag whose ban was to be immediate.

News of the disciplinary actions inevitably made it into the press. Tendulkar was one of the game's greatest batsmen and for his name to be besmirched by an allegation like this added to the outrage in India. Claims of racism were made against Denness. The Indians were unhappy that during the Test a vigorous appeal by a South African player had gone unpunished, whereas their players were being punished for a similar action.

Denness attended a press conference but didn't go into any detail to justify his decisions. He claimed that this wasn't normal procedure, but it didn't calm the situation. Protests took place in India and an effigy of Denness was burnt. Amid the furore the Indian cricket board refused to allow its players to play the third Test unless Denness was replaced. A third unofficial Test took place before which Denness was told he would not be allowed into the ground. Tendulkar's ban was overturned after it was stated his offence was not ball-tampering but cleaning the ball without informing the umpire.

DRAVID COUGHS UP

During a One Day International against Zimbabwe in 2004, India's Rahull Dravid was found applying a cough lozenge to the ball. He claimed he was cleaning it off. He was fined half his match fee.

UTTER MINTS

Australia were the Ashes holders when they came to England in 2005, confident of victory. It was a close competition, with one Test won by two runs, the smallest margin in the history of the Ashes. The series went to the very last day and saw England win the series 2–1 – their first Ashes victory for 18 years.

In 2008 England batsman Marcus Trescothick published his autobiography, *Coming Back to Me*. It contained an admission that, when England were bowling in the 2005 Ashes, he was tasked with keeping the shine on the ball. This would help keep it swinging for longer. Reverse-swing bowling had been one of the major factors in England's victory.

Trescothick used his saliva, enhanced with a brand of sweets called Murray Mints. His admission caused figures from the game to comment on the ethics – or not – of his actions. According to the rules that govern the game, no artificial substance can be applied to the ball's surface, but the ICC stated, 'According to the laws this is illegal but we won't outlaw sucking sweets.' Trescothick received no punishment.

HAIR LOSS

The fourth Test of Pakistan's tour of England in 2006 was played at the Oval. On the fourth day, umpires Darrell Hair and Billy Doctrove suspected Pakistan's players of ball-tampering and replaced the ball, awarding five penalty runs to England. This resulted in the Pakistan players refusing to continue playing after the interval in protest. The match officials awarded the game to England – the first ever Test to be won and lost by forfeiture. The considerable fallout saw umpire Darrell Hair banned from umpiring internationals and the Pakistan captain Inzamam-ul-Haq being banned for four One Day Internationals.

SPIKED

During the match against South Africa in Cape Town in 2010, English players Stuart Broad and James Anderson were accused of ball-tampering with their spikes. Broad was seen stopping the ball while fielding with his foot. He said that it was laziness in the 40-degree heat that made him not bend down. Anderson was accused of tampering with the ball's seam. No disciplinary action resulted.

ONCE BITTEN, TWICE BANNED

In 2010, Pakistan's stand-in captain Shahid Afridi was banned for two matches after being seen biting the ball while playing against Australia. He claimed he was only smelling the ball but TV cameras proved otherwise. Pakistan lost the series 5–0.

VIOLENCE

Contact sports require a certain amount of aggressive behaviour, yet occasionally this veers into violent actions that have no place in the world of sport – but that do have a place in the law courts.

KEY SCANDAL: THE BITE FIGHT

It might be strange to include a scandal featuring boxing under the category of violence, but what happened in 1997 was extraordinary.

Mike Tyson had turned professional in 1985. 'Iron Mike', as he became known, had won the World Boxing Council (WBC) heavyweight title in 1986, aged 20, the youngest ever heavyweight world champion. His first 19 professional fights were won by knockouts. In his best performance in June 1988, the 21-year-old Tyson knocked out Michael Spinks in the first round. Spinks had been unbeaten in 31 fights until this bout. (Tyson's record up to that fight was 34 wins with 30 knockouts). After his 91-second defeat, the 31-year-old Spinks never boxed professionally again.

Tyson defended his world heavyweight championship title nine times but was defeated in 1990 by James 'Buster' Douglas. In 1992 Tyson was jailed for rape and spent three years in jail. He returned to boxing and in September 1996

Tyson became World Boxing Association (WBA) heavyweight champion. A fight was agreed between Tyson and Evander Holyfield, to take place in November 1996 in Las Vegas. It was Tyson's first defence of his regained title.

It was widely assumed that Tyson would win easily. Holyfield had been WBA and International Boxing Federation (IBF) champion but had lost these titles in 1994. He then retired but returned the following year. His return had not been too successful; it included a knockout by Riddick Bowe. The TV companies were selling the game on cable on a pay-per-round basis so as not to provoke any recriminations from annoyed viewers if it ended very quickly. Holyfield emerged victorious, being able to absorb Tyson's attacks and then issue his own blows. The fight was stopped in the eleventh round.

In the June 1997 rematch, again in Las Vegas, Tyson was determined to win but his opening barrage in the first two rounds didn't have the desired effect on his opponent. Holyfield won them. At one point a gash opened up above Tyson's right eye, the result of a headbutt from Holyfield which the referee regarded as accidental.

Tyson realised he was going to lose and so engineered a way of getting out of the fight.

In the third round, in a clinch, he bit down on the top of Holyfield's right ear, severing a one-inch-long piece of cartilage. The referee Mills Lane warned Tyson if he did it again he would be disqualified. He did it again, this time on Holyfield's left ear. Tyson was disqualified.

He was fined $3 million and had his boxing licence taken away, but this was later reinstated.

Tyson claimed he did it in retaliation against headbutting from his opponent in both fights, saying: 'He butted me in the second round and he butted me again. He kept butting me and nobody would help me. This is my career. What am I supposed to do? I've got children to raise.'

Tyson retired in 2006. Despite taking part in some of the most lucrative fights of all time, and earning an estimated $400 million, he had filed for bankruptcy in 2003.

THE BUTCHER OF SEVILLE

In the 1982 football World Cup, France and Germany had progressed to the semi-final stage, where they met in Seville on 8 July. Germany had advanced via the scandal of their game against Austria that helped to oust Algeria (see Load of Hrubesch on page 47).

The score was 1–1 in the fifty-seventh minute when a well-hit through ball by French midfield general Michel Platini was chased by Patrick Battiston. West German goalkeeper Harald Schumacher came running out to meet him. Battiston got to the ball first and directed it towards goal from just outside the penalty box. It slipped feet-wide. The 6-feet-1-inch Schumacher had continued his run and jumped up, turning away in mid-air to hit the Frenchman in the head with his hip. Battiston fell to the ground inside the penalty box, unconscious. He was carried off and given oxygen before being taken to hospital. He was so pale, Platini thought he was dead. Battiston lost three teeth, and suffered a cracked vertebra and three cracked ribs. While the Frenchman lay immobile on the pitch, Schumacher stood with the ball placed, ready to take the goal kick that the referee had awarded.

There was no sending off for Schumacher, which would have been the obvious outcome to anyone who had seen what he'd done. But crucially neither the referee nor the linesmen had. Play continued.

The game went on to end 3–3 after Germany came back from being 3–1 behind. They won the penalty shoot-out. Schumacher saved two of the kicks. It is safe to assume it wasn't just Italians cheering when Germany lost the final to Italy.

The fallout was tremendous, but Schumacher did not appear too contrite. He was criticised by his own football federation, who regretted his attitude and comments he made: the German had offered to pay Battiston's dental bills. Schumacher was subsequently dubbed by French fans 'The Butcher of Seville'. A German newspaper felt so bad about the incident that it offered Battiston a free week's holiday.

In 2014 Battiston said he had forgiven the German for his assault. He said, 'We will never know if it was deliberate or not. Over time I have come to realise people have forever marked him with this.'

CLOUGH'S OFF

Brian Clough was one of British football's most colourful figures. As a player he was noted for his goals, but it was his time as a manager with Peter Taylor as his assistant that he will be mostly remembered for. He took Derby from the English Second Division into the First Division and then to the League title in 1972.

He then had a disastrous spell at Leeds United, where the players were not enamoured with him, his comments about them or his methods. He left after 44 days. This led the way to the club he would manage for almost 20 years: Nottingham Forest. He took over in 1975 and took this Second Division club to the top of the First Division and then to the highest level in Europe by winning the European Cup in 1979 and 1980.

In 1989, Nottingham Forest were playing Queens Park Rangers in a Littlewoods Cup quarter-final. They ended the match 5–2 winners and some of their fans ran on to the pitch to celebrate. Clough confronted some, shouting for them to get off the pitch. He even lashed out, landing blows on several of the fans.

Some of these fans were identified and spoke to the media. One of them, Paul Richardson, denied they were hooligans, saying: 'The only person on the pitch that was a hooligan that night was Brian Clough.' Another, Sean O'Hara, described Clough 'swinging around like a madman with his fists'.

But Clough was not handed any assault charges; indeed the opposite was the case. He had widespread backing for his unorthodox crowd-control methods. Forest's chairman Maurice Roworth later stated that they had received 679 letters about the incident and 628 were supportive of the manager. One of the letters was from the leader of the Labour Party, Neil Kinnock. The FA, however, took a dim view and issued Clough with a touchline ban for three months and fined him £5,000.

Clough issued a statement regretting his actions. A few days after the game, two of the fans were invited to the ground and – showing the magnetic power of their club's manager – made to apologise on TV.

Clough retired in 1993 after Forest were relegated.

DUNCAN DISORDERLY

You Nutter!

News of the World headline, 17 April 1994

Striker Duncan Ferguson began his professional career with Dundee United. His record of 34 goals in 86 games saw him bought by Rangers in the summer of 1993 for £4 million, which was a record British transfer fee at the time. He made only a handful of appearances for the Glasgow club before being loaned to English club Everton in October 1994. Before that, however, came the incident that was to secure his place in sporting infamy.

On 16 April 1994, Rangers were at home to Raith Rovers. Ferguson scored his first goal for the club in an eventual 4–0 win. As well as striking the ball into the net, he also struck his own forehead into that of Raith's John McStay. In the thirty-fifth minute the two were tussling for the ball in one of the corners of the pitch. It seemed that McStay was about to emerge with the ball at his feet when he was held back by Ferguson. McStay stopped, turned and then the 6-feet-4-inches-tall Ferguson lowered his head and landed his forehead on the defender's face. The referee Kenny Clark didn't see it and Ferguson stayed on the pitch.

TV and photographers' cameras had caught it, however, and this was to have serious consequences for Ferguson as he was on probation after a conviction for assault in August 1993 following a fracas in an Anstruther pub. This conviction followed two others: in 1991 Ferguson was fined £125 for butting a policeman and in 1992 was fined £200 for assaulting a postman on crutches after he'd taunted Ferguson and insulted his girlfriend. This incident came on the same day Ferguson had been sent off for the first time, for a headbutt on St Johnstone player John Inglis.

The Procurator Fiscal charged Ferguson with assault – the first time an on-field sporting incident had led to legal prosecution in Britain. Ferguson was convicted and given three months, reduced to 44 days on appeal, in Glasgow's infamous Barlinnie Prison.

The Scottish Football Association had also got involved and banned the striker for 12 games before the trial took place. This angered Ferguson, who felt they should have waited until after the court case. Having made his international debut in 1992 against the USA, and going on to appear six more times for his nation, he never played for Scotland again.

Ferguson was later signed by Everton for £4 million and became a fans' favourite during his two spells as a player at the club. He became first-team coach at Everton in February 2014.

In 2003, Ferguson's Merseyside house was broken into by a burglar who had to receive hospital treatment after being confronted. This followed another burglary in 2001 when two men broke into his house in west Lancashire. One of them was restrained by Ferguson, before being arrested by the police and spending three days in hospital.

ANDRÉS ESCOBAR

Thanks for the own goal.

Colombia had gone to the 1994 World Cup in the USA with high hopes. These hopes were severely dented when, in their group game against the hosts, they scored an own goal. In the twenty-second minute Colombian captain Andrés Escobar stretched out his foot to intercept the ball as it was crossed into the penalty box. He connected with the ball but instead of putting it behind for a corner, he directed it into the net. It was his first professional own goal. The Americans went on to win 2–1 and Colombia were eliminated from the tournament.

Colombia had not played to their potential in the tournament, especially in light of how they qualified, which included a 5–0 defeat of Argentina. They had lost only once in 26 matches before the tournament and Brazilian legend Pelé had tipped Colombia to win the World Cup. However, in their first game they lost 3–1 to Romania, before the disastrous defeat by the USA. In their last game, when they were already eliminated, they regained some form to beat Switzerland 2–0.

Days after returning home, Escobar was in a bar in Medellín when some men began insulting him about his role in Colombia's exit from the World Cup. The confrontation escalated as Escobar left and as he sat in his car he was shot six times. It was before he was shot that one of the attackers offered their sarcastic comment, 'Thanks for the own goal'.

Whether he was killed as a result simply of the confrontation or of something more sinister remains unknown. There were rumours that the game had been target of large-scale betting, and criminal gangs were unhappy about the shock defeat for the South American side. The players had received death threats before the USA game. Furthermore, when the squad were all threatened with being murdered if Gabriel 'Barrabas' Gómez played, he was left out of the team. He then withdrew from the squad.

Escobar was invited to remain in the USA after his team's exit, but he had insisted he wanted to go home. After his team's departure from the World Cup he had written in a Colombian newspaper, 'Life doesn't end here. We have to go on.'

ICE BREAKING

Why? Why? Why?
Nancy Kerrigan, 6 January 1994

If thinking of a sport performed on ice that features violence, it's usually ice hockey that comes to mind. Women's figure skating would not rank highly on any list, until perhaps the events of January 1994.

Nancy Kerrigan and Tonya Harding were American figure skaters who competed in the early 1990s. Harding made history by being the first American to successfully perform a triple axel jump, on her way to becoming US champion in 1991. The two were also competing against Kristi Yamaguchi, but when Yamaguchi turned professional at the end of the 1991–2 season the way was clear for them to vie for the top spot.

It was on 6 January 1994 that matters took the violent turn that was to gain worldwide interest. Kerrigan had just finished a practice session for the US Championships and was making her way through the backstage area when a masked assailant hit her in the right leg with a police baton. She was filmed being tended to by first-aid workers, the microphone picking up her plaintive cries of 'Why? Why? Why?' As a result of her injuries she had to withdraw from the championships. Harding won.

To some it appeared as if her rival had been nobbled to ensure Harding's victory. And so it turned out. In 1990, aged 19, Harding had married Jeff Gillooly. The couple divorced three years later, but got back together soon after. Before the US Championships, Gillooly orchestrated a plan to ensure his wife would be assured of a gold medal in the forthcoming Winter Olympics. He hired in help: Harding's bodyguard Shawn Eckhardt, getaway car driver Derrick Smith and Smith's nephew, Shane Stant. Stant and Smith gained access to the ice skating rink in Detroit where Kerrigan was practising. They had planned to cut her Achilles tendon or run her car off the road, or even kill her, but settled on breaking her leg. Gillooly reasoned that as the right was Kerrigan's landing leg this was the best target for their attack.

Not long after the assault, the FBI were tipped off. They moved quickly and, after Eckhardt confessed, all four men involved were found guilty and given jail sentences in the summer of 1994. The question remained: how much did Harding know? She had protested innocence about the plot (a position she maintains to this day) but was given probation for obstructing the prosecution. Her ex-husband Gillooly claimed she did know about it beforehand.

Despite not taking part in the qualifying tournament – the assailants had failed to break her leg but had inflicted a serious injury – Kerrigan was picked for the Winter Olympics to be held in February at Lillehammer in Norway, along with Harding. The two were the subject of much public and media attention. The much-hyped battle was an anti-climax: Kerrigan won silver but Harding was eighth, after suffering a broken lace in one of her performances. Kerrigan retired from amateur skating after the Olympics. Harding was banned for life and became a professional boxer.

In an interview with *Deadspin* in 2013, Gillooly said about Harding: 'We decided to do something really stupid there, and it ruined her. She'll never be remembered for how wonderful a figure skater she was.'

BEASTED

In 1994 the All Blacks rugby team were hosting South Africa in a three-match Test series. Following a 13–9 victory in the second Test in Wellington, the All Blacks clinched the series, but the game would be remembered for more than their victory.

During the game the All Blacks' captain Sean Fitzpatrick told referee Brian Stirling that he had had his ear bitten. Stirling and his touch judges hadn't seen the incident which took place during a ruck and so no action was taken during the game but the culprit wasn't about to get away with it: TV cameras had recorded South Africa prop Johan Le Roux biting Fitzpatrick's ear.

Le Roux – nicknamed 'The Beast' – was sent home in disgrace and banned for 18 months. He missed the World Cup, which was won by his own country. He said: 'For an 18-month suspension, I feel I probably should have torn it off. Then at least I could say: "Look, I've returned to South Africa with the guy's ear."'

Le Roux had previous form when it came to dishing out on-field pain. A couple of months before his nibble at Fitzpatrick's ear, he had put England player Martin Johnson out of action with one punch. Fearing concussion, Johnson flew home and was replaced on the tour.

After his 18-month suspension was up, Le Roux returned to play and in his second match back was suspended for seven weeks after headbutting an opponent.

CANTONA KICKS OFF

It might be a cliché to suggest that Eric Cantona was 'mercurial', but it would be difficult to find a better word to describe this Frenchman who lived by his own rules. He was certainly not the model of a Premiership footballer.

Born in 1966, he had played in France for a number of clubs before arriving in England, signing for Leeds in 1991. With this skilful forward in the side, the Yorkshire club won their first league title for 18 years. Manchester United manager Alex Ferguson made a cheeky move for the player and was surprised when Leeds sold him for £1.2 million in November 1992. The journey westwards across the Pennines was to transform the Manchester club's fortunes. In his first season, Cantona helped the Red Devils win the league, their first for 26 years.

However, there had always been signs in Cantona's game that his temper could flare up. He was convicted of spitting at Leeds United fans when returning to their Elland Road ground in February 1993, and while playing in France he had threatened to retire from football after being banned for a month. The crime? Throwing a ball at the referee.

His anger was to land him in bigger trouble in his third season at Old Trafford.

The game was on 25 January 1995, with Manchester United away to Crystal Palace. United went ahead but Gareth Southgate equalised with 11 minutes to go. The game ended a 1–1 draw. However, that was almost completely ignored when put against the events that took place just after half-time. Cantona was heavily tackled by Palace's Richard Shaw. He retaliated, kicking him. The referee showed him the red card and Cantona began walking off the pitch. (It was his fifth sending off in 16 months.) A Palace fan ran down the stand's steps towards the touchline, gesturing and shouting abuse, reportedly suggesting the Frenchman should 'f**k off back to France'. Before anyone realised what was happening, Cantona leapt at the man, flying through the air with both feet first. He then threw a few punches.

There was outrage. Cantona was convicted in court of assault on the Crystal Palace fan and sentenced to two weeks in prison, although on appeal this was later reduced to 120 hours of community service. At a subsequent press conference, he famously said only one thing to the media before leaving: 'When the seagulls follow the trawler, it's because they think sardines will be thrown into the sea.'

The Football Association fined him £10,000 and banned him from playing for eight months. Cantona lost the captaincy of the French national side and wasn't selected again, denying him the chance to lift the World Cup in 1998.

In his first game back for United, he scored a penalty in a 2–2 draw with Liverpool. In that season, his team won the Premier League and FA Cup double. Cantona scored a memorable goal in the final, volleying from 20 yards, the ball travelling through most of the defending Liverpool players for the only goal of the game. After winning the league title the following season he retired, aged 30. The following year Arsenal won the league title.

He had spent five years with Manchester United, and won four league titles and two FA cups. Cantona featured in several films, including Ken Loach's 2009 *Looking for Eric* in which an obsessed Manchester United fan imagined Cantona appearing – as himself – to offer advice. He says in one scene: 'I am not a man. I am Cantona.'

ROY'S KEANE

Irishman Roy Keane is commonly named in Manchester United 'greatest ever' teams. The combative midfielder was captain of the side from 1997 to 2005 and in his period at Old Trafford he won seven league titles and the FA Cup four times. Due to suspension he missed the famous 2–1 victory over Bayern Munich in the 1999 Champions League final.

Keane was known to be an aggressive player, but one moment was to stand out above all others.

In September 1997, Manchester United were playing Leeds United. During the game there was niggling between Keane and Leeds United's Norwegian midfielder Alf-Inge Håland. Manchester United were losing 1–0 and, with time running out, Keane's frustrations led to him tripping up Håland, but the Irishman came off worse. His studs stuck in the grass and he tore a cruciate ligament.

Håland was not aware of this at the time and accused Keane of play-acting. Keane missed the rest of the season and Arsenal went on to win the league.

In the summer of 2000, Håland had joined rivals Manchester City. In the Manchester derby on 21 April 2001 Keane exacted what many observers thought was revenge. Moments after Håland played the ball, Keane lunged with his right leg and put the full force of his studs on Håland's right knee, sending him spinning to the ground. Keane was sent off and later fined £5,000 and suspended for three games.

After the incident Håland played on. He retired in 2003. In 2008 he said: 'Did that tackle end my career? Well, I never played a full game again, did I? It seems like a great coincidence, don't you think?'

In August 2002, Keane's autobiography was published in which he wrote how he had wanted to hurt the Norwegian: 'I'd waited long enough. I f**king hit him hard.' The Football Association reacted to Keane's comments and fined him £150,000 and issued a five-match ban for bringing the game into disrepute.

In 2014 Keane wrote in his second autobiography *The Second Half*: 'There are things I regret in my life and he [Håland] is not one of them.'

Keane moved to Celtic in 2005, where he finished his playing career after ten appearances in the Hoops. He moved to management and was in charge of Sunderland and Ipswich Town before joining Martin O'Neill as assistant manager of the Republic of Ireland, helping take them to the European Championships of 2016.

LE COUP DE TÊTE

He's not a smooth star, he's not a nice guy. He's capable of anything and that's what makes him a human god.

Raymond Domenech, ex-France manager in *Le Monde*, January 2016

During the later 1990s and early 2000s, Zinedine Zidane was one of the world's greatest football players, whose attacking midfield prowess helped drive his club teams and national team to success.

His passing, vision and shooting ability made him a central part of any team he played in. At Juventus, where he played from 1996 to 2001, he contributed to two Serie A league titles but lost in two Champions League finals. Playing for France, Zidane was in the team that won the World Cup in 1998, where he scored two goals in the final, and then the European Championships two years later.

In 2001 he left Italy for Spain, joining Real Madrid as one of the *galacticos* (Spanish for 'superstar') with whom Real Madrid president Florentino Pérez wished to fill his team. Other *galacticos* included Portuguese winger Luís Figo, Brazilian forward Ronaldo and England's David Beckham. Zidane's move from Juventus cost the Spanish club a record sum at the time: £46 million.

In the Champions League final of 2002, held at Glasgow's Hampden Park, Zidane scored a memorable goal, volleying a Roberto Carlos cross home from just inside the penalty box.

However, alongside such sublime moments of skill, in his career Zidane had shown moments of 'the red mist' – the flashing of temper that was to result in his biggest moment of shame.

In the World Cup of 1998, he had been sent off for stamping on a Saudi Arabian player and received a two-match ban. In October 2000 when Juventus were losing to Hamburg in a Champions League group match, he had been sent off for headbutting Jochen Kientz, fracturing the German's cheek. Afterwards, Zidane said, 'I committed a dreadful foul. Anyone can lose their cool, it's human – but that's no excuse.' This game was Zidane's first after being sent off against Deportivo La Coruña in September for a rash challenge.

In 2006, Zidane's France were in the World Cup final against Italy. The game started well for Zidane, who scored a penalty in the seventh minute, after a foul on Florent Malouda in the box by Marco Materazzi. The Italian made amends for his error by equalising in the eighteenth minute. The score remained 1–1 and the game went into extra time. In the one-hundred-and-fourth minute Zidane had a glorious chance to repeat his feats in the 1998 final as he flashed a long-range header towards the goal, but Italian goalkeeper Buffon flicked the ball over the bar and Zidane shouted his frustration.

Then came the moment. As a French attack broke down, Zidane and Materazzi walked away from the box together. The play moved up the pitch. After talking for several seconds, Zidane turned and lunged, headbutting the tall Italian defender in the chest. The incident was not immediately seen and it was only when the referee's attention was called to the prone Materazzi that he became aware that something had happened. None of the two assistant referees had seen the incident but the fourth official, Luis Medina Cantalejo, had seen it and told Argentinian referee Horacio Elizondo: 'A really violent headbutt by Zidane on Materazzi, right in the chest.'

An immediate red card was issued for violent conduct by Elizondo and Zidane's last steps on a football pitch as a player were as he walked disconsolately past the tournament's trophy as it stood on a plinth.

Zidane never revealed what Materazzi had said that made him react. Straight after the game, lip-reading experts offered various explanations, from Materazzi calling Zidane's sister a whore or his mother a whore, with others thinking he'd called him a terrorist. In May 2014 the Italian revealed what he'd said. Just prior to the headbutting, when the French were attacking, Materazzi had been holding Zidane's jersey, leading the Frenchman to reportedly say to the Italian defender, 'If you really want my shirt you can have it later.' Materazzi had responded, 'I'd rather have your sister.'

BORN TOULOUSE

Rugby is a game where the occasional fist being thrown isn't regarded as anything untoward. It's a different matter when the fists are thrown at spectators.

Irishman Trevor Brennan was a forward for French club Toulouse when his team faced Ulster at home in the Heineken Cup on 21 January 2007. He had started his career at a junior club in Dublin, which led to his nickname 'the Barnhall Bruiser'.

Brennan was a substitute for the game and in the second half was warming up on the touchline. There was some good-natured banter with some in the crowd, then things turned nasty. Brennan went over the perimeter wall towards the crowd. The 6-feet-5-inches player went up some stairs and then started laying into an Ulster fan, Patrick Bamford, hitting him six or seven times, leaving him bruised and shaken.

Brennan claimed he had been subjected to abuse about his mother and also sectarian comments from the crowd, but an inquiry found this not to be the case. The Ulster fans had been slagging off the bar he owned in Toulouse, Bamford shouting that the bar was 'crap'.

After the altercation, Brennan was led away but still took part in the game, yet soon after was sin-binned for fighting with Ulster's Justin Harrison.

Brennan was fined €25,000 and given a lifetime ban from playing the game and from participating in any capacity in European Cup games, although this was later reduced to five years. He was also ordered to pay €5,000 to Bamford in damages and was fined €800 by French criminal authorities.

The 33 year old had retired from rugby before the punishments were announced.

NO ANGEL

Angel Matos, who had won gold at the Sydney Olympics in 2000, was representing Cuba in taekwondo at the Beijing Olympics eight years later. In the bronze medal bout of the +80kg competition Matos was beating Arman Chilmanov of Kazakhstan 3–2 when he required treatment for a foot injury. Unfortunately for him, this went over the one-minute limit for injury time. As a result he was immediately disqualified. Angry at this decision, he kicked out – literally – and his foot connected with the face of Swedish judge Chakir Chelbat.

Matos spat on the floor and had another go at an official as he was encouraged to leave the arena. The Cuban was not without his supporters. His coach said of the judge, 'He was too strict', and Cuban president Fidel Castro sympathised, saying: 'He could not contain himself.' The general secretary of the World Taekwondo Federation was not impressed. He said, 'It was an insult to the Olympic vision, to the spirit of taekwondo and for me an insult to mankind.' They banned Matos for life.

LUIS LUIS

Among the headbutts, punches, elbows and feet that are used to attack fellow players, there is one method that professional footballers regard as beyond the pale: biting. One player who has gained an unenviable reputation for the latter is Uruguayan Luis Suárez, so much so that it has overshadowed his great talent as a striker. When playing in the Netherlands for Ajax, Suárez bit PSV Eindhoven's Otman Bakkal in November 2010. For leaving teeth marks in Bakkal's shoulder he was subsequently banned for seven games. He was also fined by his club.

Suárez left Ajax shortly after and joined Liverpool in January 2011. Two years later he was banned for ten games after biting Branislav Ivanović of Chelsea on the arm during a league match in April 2013. Bakkal said in the aftermath of this incident, 'I think he wants to win so badly that he loses his mind sometimes but afterwards he comes to his senses.'

Suárez sank his not inconsiderable gnashers into the shoulder of Italian defender Giorgio Chiellini in his country's final group game in the 2014 World Cup in Brazil. Suárez claimed the Italian had bumped into him with his shoulder. The referee – Mexican Marco Rodríguez, appropriately nicknamed Dracula – did not see the incident and Suárez was not punished while on the pitch.

At a later hearing, he was banned from football for four months and from international matches for nine games. He was also fined 100,000 Swiss francs. In his autobiography Suarez wrote: 'I know biting appals a lot of people, but it's relatively harmless.'

In July 2014 he signed for Barcelona in a £75 million deal. He promised not to bite anyone else.

GONE FOR A BARTON

So often has Joey Barton's name appeared in the headlines, he could have a chapter of his own. The Merseysider began his professional football career at Manchester City, making his first appearance in the light-blue jersey in April 2003. Throughout his controversial career he has been ordered off the field of play several times:

Red Card #1

Barton's first red card was received during an FA Cup game against Tottenham Hotspur in February 2004. He was sent off after the whistle had been blown for half-time, with his side 3–0 down. Barton's arguing with the referee saw him shown a second yellow (his first had been for a late tackle). His team fought back to win 4–3.

In July 2004 he provoked a brawl after kicking at Doncaster Rovers player Paul Green as he attempted to shield the ball. It was a friendly match. Later that year, Barton was in serious trouble when he stubbed a lit cigar into the eye of one of City's youth players, Jamie Tandy, on the players' Christmas night out. Immediately before, Tandy had set fire to Barton's shirt. Barton was fined four weeks' wages (with an additional two suspended).

Away from football, Barton was in bother in May 2005 when he broke a pedestrian's leg while driving at night through Liverpool, and in July the same year he was sent home from a pre-season tournament in Thailand after being involved in a fracas in a hotel after a 15-year-old Everton supporter kicked him in the shin. During the confusion Barton bit the hand of his teammate, captain Richard Dunne. He was fined eight weeks' wages by his club. As a result of this, Barton was advised to receive anger-management therapy.

Red Card #2

In February 2006 Barton was sent off against Liverpool after two bookable offences. And in September 2006 he was fined £2,000 by the FA for bringing the game into disrepute after flashing his backside at Everton fans during a game at the Liverpool club's Goodison Park.

Red Card #3

Barton was sent off for a two-footed tackle on Abdoulaye Faye of Bolton Wanderers in December 2006.

In May 2007 he was suspended and fined £100,000 by his club after an assault on teammate Ousmane Dabo that left

Dabo unconscious. This wasn't the end of his punishment. He was charged with assault and in July 2008 was given a four-month suspended prison sentence. As well as having to perform 200 hours of community service, he was ordered to pay £3,000 compensation to Dabo. The FA banned him for six games – with another six-game ban suspended – and fined him £25,000.

Barton was transferred to Newcastle United in the summer of 2007. Following a derby game against Sunderland, he was criticised for going in feet-high against Dickson Etuhu yet he received no punishment.

In May 2008 he was given a jail sentence of six months for an assault on a man and a teenager in Liverpool in December 2007. He was released in July after serving 74 days for what the judge called a 'violent and cowardly act'. Barton punched the man around 20 times and then attacked the 16 year old, breaking his teeth.

Red Card #4

In May 2009 Barton was sent off for a late tackle on Liverpool's Xabi Alonso. Following this match Barton was involved in a training ground bust-up with manager Alan Shearer and his assistant Iain Dowie. As a result Barton was suspended by the club.

In November 2010 Barton punched Blackburn's Morten Gamst Pedersen in the chest, for which he was banned for three matches by the FA.

In 2011 he moved south to London to play for Queens Park Rangers and was made captain by manager Neil Warnock.

Red Card #5

Barton was sent off for headbutting Norwich's Bradley Johnson in January 2012.

Red Card #6

In the final match of the season in May 2012, QPR were away to Barton's old club Manchester City. In the fifty-fifth minute Barton was sent off for elbowing Carlos Tevez. This wasn't the end of Barton's violent conduct on the pitch: he kicked Sergio Agüero and tried to headbutt Vincent Kompany. He was given a 12-match ban and fined £75,000 by the FA. His club fined him six weeks' wages and he lost the captaincy.

In August 2012 he joined Marseille on loan. Being away from England didn't mean he was away from trouble. In May 2013 he was given a two-match suspended ban for calling Paris Saint-Germain player Thiago Silva an 'overweight ladyboy' on social media site Twitter.

Red Card #7

Barton was sent off in a game against Nancy in February 2013. He had been booked twice in the space of five minutes.

After his time abroad he returned to QPR in the summer of 2013.

Red Card #8

Barton was sent off in December 2013 against Leicester City for two yellow-card offences: elbowing a Leicester player and then moments later for dissent after being given the first yellow card.

Red Card #9
In February 2015 he was sent off for pushing a Hull defender and then hitting another player in the groin.

In August 2015 he moved to Burnley on a one-year deal, helping the Lancashire club to win the Championship in the 2015–16 season.

FAKING IT

One of the more popular methods of cheating is faking, whether it's injury, age, how many of the 26 miles in a marathon an athlete has run, or any of the other tactics shown here. The history of fakery goes back a long way...

KEY SCANDAL: INTENSE SIMULATION

The Brazilian footballer Rivaldo was known for his skill and ability to score spectacular goals. This left-footed attacking midfielder was also prolific. At club side Barcelona he scored 136 goals in 253 games.

At the World Cup in 2002, hosted jointly by South Korea and Japan, he tarnished his reputation with an action officially termed 'simulation' – the faking of injury to get another player in trouble.

The match was a group game, Brazil against Turkey. Towards the end, Rivaldo stood at the corner flag about to take a corner kick. Turkish defender Hakan Ünsal whacked the ball towards him and it hit the Brazilian in the thigh. He immediately fell to the ground, clutching his face. The South Korean referee Kim Young-Joo showed Ünsal the red card.

The referee came in for much criticism, with Haluk Ulusoy, president of the Turkish football authority, bringing up Turkey's involvement in the Korean War to castigate him: 'We sacrificed 1,000 soldiers here to defend the South Koreans and one Korean has now killed 70 million Turks. We love Koreans, but that man cannot be a referee.'

As well as the public ridicule, Rivaldo was punished by FIFA, who fined him 11,500 Swiss francs (£5,100), which was not a great deal of money to a footballer in 2002. Brazil went on to win the World Cup, beating Germany 2–0. Rivaldo retired from international football in 2003. He said after the incident that brought shame on him, 'I'm not a player who fakes fouls.'

A BUNCH OF FAKERS

In 1898 details were published in *The Sportsman* newspaper of a horse racing meet to be held at Trodmore in Cornwall on the first bank holiday in August. One of the horses due to run in the fourth race was called Reaper. On the day of the meet, the results were sent to *The Sportsman*. Reaper had come first, at 5/1. Some bookmakers wouldn't pay out as the results hadn't been published in the other sports paper of the day, *The Sporting Life*.

The gentleman who had arranged the details to be first published, a Mr G. Martin, then contacted *The Sporting Life* and the winners and their prices were subsequently printed. It was then that an error was spotted. The starting price for Reaper was given as 5/2 and not 5/1. When bookmakers tried to contact the racecourse to confirm the price, they discovered that there was no racecourse at Trodmore and indeed there was no actual place in Cornwall called Trodmore. It was all completely fabricated by Mr Martin and his associates, whom the police were subsequently unable to track down. It was estimated that the fakers made £100,000.

LORZ OF THE RINGS

St Louis was the venue for the 1904 Olympic Games, the first time they had been held in the USA. The marathon was the event that gained most publicity – and this was in a games where a man with a wooden leg won three golds in the gymnastic competition. Those taking part were a mixture of serious marathon runners and... others. The others included a party of Greek men who, despite hailing from the country where the race originated, had never run one. Also involved were two South Africans who were part of the World's Fair being held in the city at the same time and who raced barefoot, and a former postman from Cuba who had to hitchhike to St Louis after losing all his money gambling. Among the serious runners was Fred Lorz, who had come fifth in the Boston Marathon earlier in the year.

It was a hot and humid day and the dusty course included seven hills. The athletes were not running in a closed-off area – they had to avoid traffic and pedestrians as they made their way round the 24.85-mile course. The runners were accompanied by a number of cars, which unhelpfully kicked dust up and into their lungs. In these conditions the competitors also struggled to secure water, because the race organisers did not provide them with much, as they were interested in research on dehydration. Only two water stations were set up, at six and 12 miles.

Another hazard was dogs: one of the South African athletes had to make a mile detour after being chased by a pack of wild mutts.

One of the runners, William Garcia, suffered with internal bleeding due to the dust tearing his stomach lining and he had to be taken to hospital, narrowly surviving with his life. Meanwhile, Cuban runner Félix (also known as Andarin) Carvajal, who was running in street shoes and a beret, suffered stomach cramps from eating peaches and rotten apples, and had to have a lie down. Others succumbed to cramps of the leg kind.

Fred Lorz had been in front from the start but was soon overtaken by Thomas Hicks. Lorz stopped running at the nine-mile mark. And got a lift in a car. With seven miles to go Hicks' support team, rather than giving him water, provided him with a cocktail of egg whites and strychnine. Commonly used as a poison, in tiny doses it was a performance stimulant. There were no anti-doping laws in place in 1904.

After an 11-mile journey in the car, Lorz felt fit enough to continue. He rejoined the race – in the lead – and ran into the stadium before having the winner's wreath placed on his head. Officials out on the course had seen him in the car and disqualified him but he ran on regardless. Lorz claimed his pretending to have run the whole race was just a joke. He was the first athlete to be disqualified for cheating and received a life ban, but this was later rescinded and he legitimately won the 1905 Boston Marathon.

Hicks entered the stadium 16 minutes behind Lorz. He had been given a second dose of strychnine along with a measure of brandy. His passage to the end of the race was not graceful but a slow progression as he stumbled, experienced hallucinations and was desperate to lie down. Hicks said, 'Never in my life have I run such a tough course. The terrific hills simply tear a man to pieces.'

ROAD TO RUIZ

Rosie Ruiz 'won' the 1980 Boston Marathon by missing out the first 25 miles and only running in part of the last one. Unsurprisingly, she set a course record time. Her ruse was seen through easily, as eyewitnesses stated she ran on to the course after emerging from the crowd with half a mile to the finish. There were no photographs or footage of her on the course and no athlete had seen her running. She was stripped of her win. Ruiz had qualified for Boston by completing the New York marathon, but a photographer remembered seeing her on the New York subway during the race. After Ruiz's disqualification, the finish of the race was restaged, allowing the second-placed runner, Jacqueline Gareau from Canada, to be photographed as the rightful winner.

GOODNIGHT, RAPID VIENNA

Celtic have a proud history of competing in European competitions, headed by their famous victory in the European Cup in 1967, when they became the first British football club to win that trophy. Their ground at Parkhead in Glasgow is regarded as a special place on European nights for the atmosphere, yet on a night in November 1984 the electric ambience was to turn rancorous.

Celtic had been drawn against Rapid Vienna. In the first leg, in a game described by Celtic goalkeeper Pat Bonner as 'a nasty, niggly affair' that saw striker Alan McInally sent off, the Austrian team had won 3–1. In the return match, the Scottish team turned on their traditional attacking style and won 3–0 with goals by Brian McClair, Murdo MacLeod and Tommy Burns. The last goal saw the Rapid players surround the referee, protesting about what they saw as dangerous play by Burns in sliding in for the ball near the hands of the goalkeeper Herbert Feurer. Celtic's goal-scorer Burns was then punched in the back of the head by Austrian defender Reinhard Kienast, who was sent off.

The atmosphere was now highly charged as Rapid Vienna faced exit from the competition, being 4–3 behind on aggregate. A Celtic through ball was chased by Tommy Burns, but as the Rapid Vienna goalkeeper collected it, he stuck a leg out into the stomach of the Celtic midfielder. A penalty was awarded. However, it would be some minutes before it could be taken...

The referee's attention was drawn to a bottle that had been thrown onto the pitch from the part of Celtic's ground known as 'The Jungle'. It landed on the grass and was picked up. Then another bottle was thrown from the crowd. It also landed on the pitch but Rapid Vienna defender Rudolf Weinhofer fell to the ground as if it had connected.

Afterwards, UEFA fined Celtic £4,000 and Rapid Vienna £5,000, but the Austrian club appealed. In his report the official UEFA observer said that Weinhofer hadn't been hit by a bottle but Rapid Vienna changed their statements and claimed it was another type of object. UEFA doubled the Austrian side's fine, but also punished Celtic by ordering the match to be replayed – more than 100 miles away from Glasgow.

Manchester United's ground Old Trafford was selected. The game in December was no advert for football, with fans taking out their frustrations on the Austrians. Goalkeeper Feurer was attacked in his own net by one Celtic fan and Vienna's Peter Pacult received a kick in the groin as he came

off the pitch, but it was Celtic
in the cojones: they lost 1–0 and
Rapid Vienna progressed to the fina
by Everton.

Celtic manager Davie Hay later sai
allowed to prosper.'

NOT SWEET SIXTEEN

Scotland's international football team has never got beyond the group stages of any tournament, be it the World Cup or European Championships. So when a team progressed to the next stages in the 1989 Under-16 World Cup there was much excitement. Added to that, the tournament was being held in Scotland. In the quarter-finals they beat East Germany and then in the semi-finals put a Portugal team featuring future Real Madrid star Luis Figo out of the tournament.

The Scots had reached their first-ever World Cup final. They faced a Saudi Arabian team, but doubts had been raised about the eligibility of some of the Saudi players, especially those with moustaches.

The final was played in front of over 51,000 fans at Hampden Park, showing the level of support among the home fans, keen to see their team achieve victory. (The semi-final against Portugal was played at a bursting-at-the-seams Tynecastle in Edinburgh in front of over 30,000 fans.)

It was not to be. There was to be gutting disappointment as Scotland were pegged back from being 2–0 up. The game ended 2–2 and a penalty shoot-out saw Saudi Arabia win 5–4.

Former Scottish Football Association secretary Ernie Walker said in 2012, 'I mean, it was so obvious – the Saudi keeper

Peter Shilton.' He claimed that an unnamed
coach told him one of the Saudi players was a captain
in the Saudi army, was married and had three children.

MEXICAN'T PLAY

In the 1990 football World Cup finals in Italy, teams such as
Brazil, Germany, England, Scotland and Argentina lined up.
One team that was missing was Mexico. It wasn't that they'd
failed to qualify: their non-appearance was down to a scandal
concerning their youth team.

In 1988 Mexico's Under-20 team played in a tournament for
the Confederation of North, Central American and Caribbean
Association Football (CONCACAF) teams, to determine who
would qualify for the 1989 World Youth Championship, to be
held in Saudi Arabia. The Mexicans topped their first round
group and then in the final groupings came second to Costa
Rica. Both went through and would play in Saudi Arabia the
next year.

However, a Mexican journalist found evidence in a football
yearbook that some of the players were not under the
stipulated age barrier. Other media outlets followed the story,
which was denied by the Mexican football authorities, but
further investigation found four players were overage. One
of them, captain Aurelio Rivera, was four years over the limit
when he played.

Mexico were banned from the World Youth Championships
and replaced by the USA. Officials were given lifetime bans
and the senior team was barred from any international
competition for two years. This meant they were unable
to play in the 1988 Olympics or the 1990 World Cup. For a

football-keen country that had hosted the World Cup in 1970 and 1986, this was a humiliating blow.

CONDOR DOWNED

In the qualifying rounds for the 1990 football World Cup, Brazil were in the same group as Chile and Venezuela. When Chile went to Brazil's Maracanã stadium on 3 September 1989, they knew that a draw would see them through at the expense of their opponents, courtesy of a better goal difference. Brazil had to win to ensure their qualification, to continue their sequence of appearing in every World Cup that had been held.

Brazil went ahead with a goal in the forty-ninth minute and seemed on course for qualification. In the middle of the second half, a flare was thrown onto the pitch and Chilean goalkeeper Roberto Rojas – nicknamed the 'Condor' – fell to the ground. By the time the TV cameras picked him up there was blood streaming from his head. Rojas was carried off and the game was abandoned.

The repercussions would be serious for Brazil, with disqualification a possibility, but luckily a photographer had captured the moment the flare hit the ground: feet away from Rojas. It was revealed that the Condor had hidden a razor blade in his glove for such an eventuality. Rojas was given a lifetime ban and his country were excluded from the next World Cup in 1994.

FAILED LANDING

At Louisiana's Delta Downs racetrack on 11 January 1990, race fans who had backed Landing Officer were pleased when he romped home 24 lengths ahead of the rest of the field. At 23/1, it was a good win for the punters.

The conditions were not great for witnessing such a win, but were certainly good for orchestrating one. The thick fog meant that Landing Officer's jockey, the flamboyantly named Sylvester Carmouche, had saved his horse from the rigours of racing by sitting out most of the race, unseen in the fog and then heading off when he heard the other horses approaching. Other jockeys complained that they hadn't seen the horse during the entirety of the race. At a subsequent hearing Carmouche was banned from racing for ten years.

COME IN, NUMBER 62

After the 26 miles and 285 yards of the 1991 Brussels Marathon, Abbes Tehami was first across the line. It would have been selfish if the Algerian had savoured the moment on his own as he hadn't run the whole distance himself. The man who had started the race sporting the 62 number was his coach, Bensalum Hamiani, who ran the first seven and a half miles then after a quick handover in some nearby woods, gave the number to Tehami, who ran the rest of the race.

There was a basic flaw in their plan, which was spotted by the race organiser Milou Blavier, who said, 'They looked about the same. Only, one had a moustache.'

DIA STRAITS

Graeme Souness was the consummate midfield player, able to control games with his accurate passing, tough tackling and long-range shooting ability. He was captain of Liverpool during the early 1980s when league titles and success in

Europe were commonplace for the Merseyside club. Souness was also one of the few British players to appear in Serie A when he signed for Sampdoria in 1984.

After retiring he turned to management and led Rangers through their late-1980s revival. He left the Scottish club for Liverpool and then Galatasaray, before returning to England to manage Southampton.

In November 1996 Souness received a phone call from George Weah, the Liberian striker who had played for AC Milan in Seria A. Former World Footballer of the Year, Weah suggested Souness sign his Senegalese cousin, Ali Dia. He told him that Dia had played international football for Senegal and club football in France for Paris Saint-Germain.

Without doing too much checking up on the player, Souness signed him on a month's contract. To the surprise of the Southampton players, who didn't think much of Dia in training, Souness listed him as a substitute for a game against Leeds United.

In the first half, Matthew Le Tissier went off injured and Dia got his chance. Unfortunately for him and Souness's reputation, it was a chance to show how poor he was. He ran about, seemingly not in any given position, and was substituted after 22 minutes on the pitch.

It turned out that the caller hadn't been George Weah but a friend of Dia's and that Dia had only played in short spells in France, Finland and Germany at lower-league clubs.

Dia's contract was torn up and he went on to play for Gateshead in the GM Vauxhall Conference league. When the reality of his playing career was exposed in a local newspaper article, Dia responded by saying, 'I have been portrayed as a con man and a poor player, but I am neither and intend to prove people wrong.' Following a match where Dia went on as a substitute but was pulled off after less than 20 minutes, the manager Jim Platt described him as 'absolutely hopeless'.

Souness left Southampton at the end of that season.

FIKA THE FAKER

Sergio and Fika Motsoeneng were twins, although not identical. In the 1999 Comrades ultramarathon in South Africa they schemed to win the race by sharing the running. They used toilets along the route to swap places until Sergio was left to finish the race. Despite having someone to share the load, he came ninth. Fellow competitor Nick Bester suspected something was amiss and found his evidence on Sergio's wrist. In some photographs taken during the race 'Sergio' had a yellow watch, in others, it was pink. The watch also seemed to swap wrists. The pair were banned from the race for ten years. In 2010 Sergio tried again and finished third. He was unable to enjoy his prize money as he tested positive for a banned substance. His lawyer said in 1999, 'If he harnessed the energy he put into cheating into running the race properly, who knows, he might have finished among the top five.'

THE BERLIN WALL

In the 2000 Berlin Marathon, 33 runners were disqualified after it was found they had not run the full distance. They all started the race but didn't cross all the timekeeping checkpoints, which are situated every 3 miles around the course. Most of the runners reappeared on the system after the 15-mile mark, while others popped up again after 24 miles. Three of the runners ran to the first checkpoint at 3 miles, then were not registered on the course until the finish. It appeared that Berlin's subway system was the method of transportation rather than their own feet. The current instructions for runners taking part in the race advise that travel on the subway is free for runners 'but only for those who have dropped out of the race'.

NO ID

At the 2000 Paralympics, Spain celebrated as their basketball ID team won the gold. ID stood for intellectual disabilities, that is, for athletes whose IQ was lower than 70.

A few days after the event, one of the team members, Carlos Ribagorda, sent his medal back to the games' organisers. He stated that he was one of the ten members of the team who had no intellectual disability. He revealed he was actually a journalist who had been able to join the team without any sort of test to verify his eligibility.

The team's advantage was clear to see: they had been ordered to ease off in their first game as they were making it look too easy and went on to win their preliminary group stage as the only team not to lose a game. Their points for/against were 254/126.

Before their victorious return to Spain, the basketball players had been told to grow beards and wear hats and sunglasses to avoid being too recognisable but their photographs were already published. The game was up after Ribagorda's revelations and the ten who had cheated were ordered to hand back their medals. The Spanish Paralympic head,

Fernando Martin Vicente, initially denied any wrongdoing, saying, 'I am completely sure that no fraud has existed. All athletes have undergone the appropriate controls.' He later resigned when it was clear they had not.

The wider repercussions of the scandal saw the removal of intellectual disability events from Paralympic Games.

LITTLE LEAGUE, BIG TROUBLE

Danny Almonte gained much attention in August 2001 when he struck out 62 out of the 72 batters in the 2001 Little League World Series, a baseball competition open to players aged 12 or under.

Almonte, who had moved from the Dominican Republic to New York in 2000, led his team to third place in the World Series, held at South Williamsport, Pennsylvania. His ability to throw the ball at speeds of over 70 miles an hour saw him pitch a perfect game (when no member of the batting team gets as far as first base) during the series – the first in 44 years at the championships.

Danny played for the Rolando Paulino All-Stars, nicknamed 'the Baby Bombers' because they played in the Bronx, home of the famous Major League team the New York Yankees, known as 'the Bronx Bombers'. Danny's team were given the keys to the city by Mayor Rudy Giuliani, but amid all the publicity there were suspicions about the age of the team's star player. Some teams hired private investigators and their hunches were confirmed when it was revealed by *Sports Illustrated* that Danny wasn't 12. He was 14, and therefore ineligible to play. Investigations in the Dominican Republic provided evidence that his father had produced an inaccurate birth certificate.

The Baby Bombers were stripped of their wins and their scores were wiped from the records.

The blame for the scandal lay at the door of Danny's coach Rolando Paulino and his father Felipe, who were both banned from Little League for life. Paulino had been caught in 1988 putting overage players in the Latin American Little League. The head of Little League Baseball Stephen Keener said, 'Clearly, adults have used Danny Almonte and his teammates in a most contemptible and despicable way.'

Almonte missed out on playing Major League baseball and became a coach. In 2014 he said, 'They always say that I'm the cheater guy. And they don't know the whole story.'

MADRAZO WORLD

A photographer covering the 2007 Berlin Marathon was suspicious when he snapped Roberto Madrazo crossing the line wearing a hat and a windbreaker jacket – not the typical outfit of a marathon finisher.

He alerted the race officials. Madrazo's time of 2 hours 41 minutes was looked at and found to include a section of 15km that he ran in 21 minutes. The world record for that distance is 41 minutes. The explanation? Madrazo had missed two checkpoints. The 55-year-old Mexican was disqualified for cheating. He was a politician in his home country and had run for president in 2006. Opponents had used a poster which read, 'Do you believe Madrazo? I don't either!'

BLOOD ON THE TRACKSUIT

Rugby prides itself on being a tough game, played by hard men and women who avoid the play-acting and simulation exhibited by their counterparts on the soccer pitch. It's a game where the sight of blood is not uncommon. In April 2009, in a Heineken Cup quarter-final game between English team Harlequins and Irish side Leinster, there was a bit too much blood on show.

The Irish were holding on to a 6–0 lead as the game entered its final stages. With 14 minutes left, Harlequins broke through the defence and scored a try. Influential Harlequins fly-half Nick Evans had gone off early in the second half with a thigh injury and was replaced by Chris Malone, who took the conversion, which he missed. After only being on the pitch for 22 minutes, he then went off injured with a hamstring injury and was replaced by Tom Williams. With 5 minutes left, Williams went off with a blood injury, blood dripping from his mouth. This allowed the goal-kicking Evans to return. He had a chance to win the match for Harlequins but his drop-goal attempt went wide. Harlequins lost 6–5.

There were immediate suspicions. As Williams walked off the pitch, the Leinster bench made it known they didn't believe the blood was real. TV footage seemed to show Williams winking as he left the pitch.

An investigation found that a capsule containing fake blood had been given to Williams by the club's physiotherapist, which was hidden in his sock until the right moment when it was then bitten into. The capsules had been bought by the physiotherapist from a joke shop in London's Clapham Junction.

In order to make his 'injury' look authentic, once inside the dressing room Williams' lip was cut by the club doctor using a scalpel. During the investigation it was found to be not a unique occurrence. Under their director of rugby Dean Richards, Harlequins had faked blood injuries four times.

The fallout of Bloodgate's attempted duplicity was as follows:

Harlequins rugby club	Fined £259,000
Tom Williams	Suspended for 4 months
Steph Brennan (physiotherapist)	Banned for 2 years
Dr Wendy Chapman (club doctor)	Suspended by General Medical Council
Dean Richards, director of rugby	Resigned, banned for 3 years
Charles Jillings, club chairman	Resigned

BRADMAN BADMAN

Cricketer Dermot Reeve was an English all-rounder who played in three Tests and 29 One Day Internationals. He also captained Warwickshire to three major trophy wins. In 2009 he was accused of selling, as genuine, fake signatures by legendary Australian batsman Don Bradman. Reeve was using a well-known online auction website to sell signatures which he himself had authenticated.

An expert in Bradman memorabilia stated that he thought the signatures were fake. Chris Anderson, who provided advice on the authenticity of items to the Bradman Museum in New South Wales, said: 'They are very poor simulations of a genuine Bradman signature.' Reeve stopped selling the items but explained that it was because he was running out of stock.

RACISM

Sport is a part of society, and racist views regrettably find their way into the sporting arena, as with any other activity, but modern audiences are not so tolerant of views that were once more common.

KEY SCANDAL: YOU DON'T RON RON

English football manager Ron Atkinson had overseen teams such as West Bromwich Albion, Manchester United and Atlético Madrid. In 2004 he was working as pundit for ITV when he made a racist remark about Chelsea's black player Marcel Desailly. The match had finished but Atkinson's comments were broadcast to countries in the Middle East as his microphone was still switched on. Atkinson was heard to say, 'He is what is known in some schools as a f***ing lazy thick n****r.'

When his comments were broadcast to a wider audience, Atkinson resigned immediately. He said, 'I made a stupid mistake which I regret. It left me no option but to resign. At the moment I can't believe I did it.'

Atkinson was in charge at West Bromwich Albion in the late 1970s when they played three black players on a regular basis, the first club in England to do so. Laurie Cunningham, Cyrille Regis and Brendon Batson were known as The Three Degrees, named after the pop group of the time.

BASIL D'OLIVEIRA

Basil D'Oliveira was a South African who moved to England in 1960 to play cricket. He was mixed-race and therefore barred from playing his sport in his own country as South Africa's apartheid policy excluded non-whites from certain positions in society. This policy was strongly enforced by the state.

D'Oliveira made his debut for England in 1966. England were due to tour South Africa in 1968–9 and D'Oliveira's participation became a topic of debate, with the South African government putting pressure on him not to be part of the team. When the squad was announced, his name was not included. There was outraged reaction in England, as D'Oliveira had scored a 158 in the final Ashes Test that summer, which helped England to square the series. The day the squad was announced, D'Oliveira hit 128 for his county side Worcestershire.

The Reverend David Sheppard, who had been an England player, wrote to *The Times*, and called the selectors' decision 'a dreadful mistake'. Sir Learie Constantine, the former West Indies cricketer who was a member of the British Race Relations Board, said it was 'deeply to be regretted' and 'positively suspicious'. At a rally of the South Africa's ruling National Party, the audience loudly applauded the news.

The MCC insisted his omission was on cricketing grounds, but the controversy was not over. Bowler Tom Cartwright withdrew from the squad and D'Oliveira was called up as his replacement. The South African government complained and eventually England's tour was cancelled.

THE REBEL ALLIANCE

Following the D'Oliveira Affair, South Africa became excluded from international sports such as cricket and football and events such as the Olympics. There were several attempts at breaking South Africa's sporting isolation, the most infamous being that of 'the Dirty Dozen' – a tour by English cricketers in 1982. Although efforts were made to integrate non-white players into cricket, and in 1979 the ICC sent a delegation that approved of these efforts, countries such as India, Pakistan and the West Indies refused to countenance allowing international cricket to resume there.

This did not deter the South African Cricket Union, which judged that foreign players could be enticed to play in their country: money was available. They sounded out cricketers from the West Indies to see if they would play. None would. English players, however, were not so reluctant.

In March 1982 the story broke when the players were seen arriving in South Africa. Twelve went out originally and three flew out later. The fifteen 'rebels' who played were:

Graham Gooch (captain)
Geoffrey Boycott
Mike Hendrick
Alan Knott
John Lever
Arnold Sidebottom
Derek Underwood
Bob Woolmer

Dennis Amiss
John Emburey
Geoff Humpage
Wayne Larkins
Chris Old
Les Taylor
Peter Willey

For their month's work they were reportedly paid between £40,000 and £60,000. On their return, all received three-year bans from playing international cricket. One player, John Emburey, returned to play in South Africa in 1989 and was given another three-year ban. After each ban he was selected to play for England. Emburey said about the last England tour: 'In hindsight, it was a tour that maybe shouldn't have taken place.'

Other countries also had players touring South Africa:

Sri Lanka	1982–3
West Indies	1982–3, 1983–4
Australia	1985–6, 1986–7

South Africa returned to official international competition in 1991 following the ending of the country's apartheid policy.

THE EYES DON'T HAVE IT

Sponsorship is now an important part of sport, but photographs taken for an advertisement for the sponsor of the Spanish men and women's Olympic basketball teams caused upset in 2008. Both the men and women's teams were photographed for an advert for courier company Seur, which appeared in the Spanish sports newspaper *Marca* before the Beijing games started. What caused the controversy was that the players were pictured with both hands raised and their extended index fingers pulling the sides of their eyes out, in a misguided attempt to appear 'Chinese'. The Spanish centre Pau Gasol, who played for the Los Angeles Lakers, said: 'I'm sorry if anybody thought or took it the wrong way and thought it was offensive.' The International Olympic Committee (IOC) did not appear too upset, with a spokeswoman saying: 'We understand the Spanish team intended no offence and has apologised.'

HAPPY EVRA AFTER

Liverpool were playing arch-rivals Manchester United in October 2011. During the game an incident took place when words were exchanged between Liverpool's Luis Suárez and United's Patrice Evra. In an interview after the game, Evra alleged that during the match Suárez had called him a 'negrito'.

The Football Association began an investigation and charged Suárez with using 'abusive and/or insulting words and/or behaviour' towards Evra and that this included 'reference to the ethnic origin and/or colour and/or race' of the player. The hearing took place in December and Suárez was banned for eight matches and fined £40,000.

Although Liverpool, under manager Kenny Dalglish, strongly supported Suárez, they did not appeal the punishments. Suárez justified the use of the word by saying, 'Every culture has its way of expressing itself, and that's a word people in Uruguay use all the time, whether somebody's black or not black.'

After his ban was over, Suárez made his first appearance in a game against Manchester United in February 2012. Before the match there was concern over the handshakes exchanged between the players, as this pre-match ritual had been omitted in a previous game featuring Queens Park Rangers and Chelsea, following the accusation by QPR's

Anton Ferdinand over alleged racist comments by Chelsea's John Terry.

As the Liverpool players walked down the line-up of United players, shaking their hands in turn, Suárez came to Evra. He kept moving and offered his hand to the next player, goalkeeper David de Gea. United's Rio Ferdinand, standing next to De Gea, kept his hand away from Suárez. The pre-match events did not affect Manchester United unduly, who won the match 2–1.

In the next meeting of the two clubs in September 2012, the pre-match events were not repeated as all the players shook hands with each other, but the score was repeated: Liverpool lost 2–1.

CRIMES

While many scandalous activities result in purely sporting punishments, there are some sportsmen and women whose actions lead to criminal prosecution. Despite some of these crimes being carried out away from the sporting arena, the fame of the perpetrators ensures that their association with their chosen sport is heavily featured in any reporting. As can be seen in the case of footballer Ched Evans, sport is not always prepared for how to deal with the aftermath.

KEY SCANDAL: BLADE GUNNER

Oscar Pistorius is South Africa's most famous Paralympian, known as Blade Runner because of the J-shaped prosthetics he used in sprint events.

Pistorius was 11 months old when both his legs were amputated below the knee due to a congenital absence of the fibula bones. While at school, Pistorius began sprinting and he made his first appearance at a Paralympic Games in 2004 in Athens, where he won gold in the 200m. He repeated this feat in Beijing in 2008, also winning gold in two other events: the 100m and 400m.

He was determined to compete in able-bodied events and in the 2011 World Championships he won silver in the 4×400m relay – the first Paralympian to win a medal in an able-bodied world championship athletics event. Although he did not take part in the final, he qualified for a medal for his part in his team's qualification heats.

The following year Pistorius achieved another first, becoming the first amputee athlete to run in an Olympic Games. In London he competed in the 400m and 4×400m relay. He followed this with golds in the Paralympics' 400m and 4×100m relay. He missed out on gold in the 200m, coming second to Brazil's Alan Oliveira – the first time he had been beaten in the 200m. After the race, Pistorius accused the Brazilian of having an unfair advantage by using longer blades. Pistorius had faced accusations himself of having an unfair advantage over able-bodied athletes because of his blades. He later apologised for his outburst.

The Paralympics were to be his last major athletics event, as in February 2013 – on Valentine's Day – he shot and killed his girlfriend Reeva Steenkamp. He claimed he had heard an intruder inside his home in Pretoria and, in fear, had fired four shots through the bathroom door. In a highly publicised trial he was found guilty of culpable homicide and in September 2014 was sentenced to five years in prison.

Pistorius was released from prison in October 2015, but the Appeal Court overturned the culpable homicide verdict and convicted him of murder in December that year.

LONG FELLOW, LONG STRETCH

Lester Piggott is one of horse racing's most famous figures. In a hugely successful career that started when he was 12 and lasted 47 years, 'Long Fellow' (he was 5 feet 8 inches) won the Epsom Derby nine times and rode 4,493 winners in races run in Britain. He was champion jockey 11 times and won 30 Classics. He retired as a jockey initially in 1985 to work as a trainer.

Piggott came unseated in October 1987 when he was sentenced to jail for three years for tax evasion, for which he served a year and a day. He had failed to declare £3.25 million of his income. The jockey who had won many races wearing the Queen's colours was also stripped of his OBE.

After his release he returned to racing and, aged 54, won the Breeders' Cup Mile in the USA in 1990. He finally retired as a jockey in 1995, bringing an end to what the *Guardian* called 'the most remarkable career in racing history'.

POUND STRETCHER

Roy Keane's on 50 grand a week. So was I till the police found my printing machine.

Mickey Thomas

Welsh international Mickey Thomas began his football career at Wrexham, where he played six seasons before joining Manchester United. He then played for various clubs including Everton, Chelsea and Stoke City, before rejoining Wrexham in 1991. It was while at the club, in 1993, that he was given an 18-month jail sentence for passing on forged banknotes to the team's apprentices. Around £800 had been involved.

The judge at his trial, Gareth Edwards, told him: 'Largely I think because it fitted in with your self-image as a flash and daring adventurer, you betrayed the trust of your employers and you failed in your duty as a distinguished international sportsman.'

Thomas showed a sense of humour when arriving at the court for sentencing, asking the waiting journalists if they had change from a £10 note for the telephone.

THE JUICE HAS RUN OUT

Few sports stars have had a more public descent into disgrace than ex-NFL player O. J. Simpson. Nicknamed 'The Juice', Simpson made his name playing for the Buffalo Bills and then the San Francisco 49ers, before retiring in 1979. He then worked as a TV commentator and as a movie actor, appearing in films such as *The Towering Inferno*, *Capricorn One* and *The Naked Gun* crime spoof series.

His fame was to turn to infamy in 1994 when, on the night of 12 June, Simpson's ex-wife Nicole Brown and her friend Ronald Goldman were found stabbed to death outside her home in Los Angeles. A glove was found at the crime scene, which matched one found outside Simpson's home. Both had blood on them which matched the DNA of the victims.

Simpson was charged with murder and was eventually taken into custody following a slow-speed police chase of his white Ford Bronco SUV which was covered live on TV. The Los Angeles police were wary of intervening as Simpson was holding a gun to his own head.

The subsequent trial was one of the most high profile ever seen, with intense public and media interest. The live broadcast of the jury's verdict was watched by an estimated 100 million people. Simpson was acquitted.

His time in courtrooms was not over, however, and in 1997 a civil jury found him liable for Brown and Goldman's deaths and he was ordered to pay over $33 million in damages to their families. In 2008 Simpson then faced charges for taking part in an armed robbery and kidnapping in Las Vegas. Simpson and co-accused Clarence Stewart had attempted to recover sports memorabilia that Simpson claimed had been stolen from him. He was given a jail sentence of 33 years. The guilty verdict was declared 13 years, to the day, after he was acquitted of the two murders in Los Angeles.

CANNED

Cricketer Chris Lewis was an England all-rounder who played in 32 Tests and 53 One Day Internationals. Although hugely talented – he was described as the next Ian Botham – Lewis was seen as insecure about his own potential as a player. In 1999 he was approached by an Indian businessman and offered £300,000 to encourage his teammates to underperform in the Third Test at Old Trafford against New Zealand. Lewis immediately reported the approach to the police but no convictions resulted.

Lewis's cricketing career ended in 2008 (he had retired in 2000 but returned aged 41 to play Twenty20) and it was the same year that his reputation was to be ruined. Returning from St Lucia to London's Gatwick Airport on 8 December, he was pulled aside by customs officials. In the ensuing bag search they found several cans of fruit and vegetable juice. Closer inspection revealed their contents weren't too nutritional: dissolved cocaine, worth £140,000. Despite his protestations of innocence, Lewis was found guilty in May 2009 and jailed for 13 years. He was released in June 2015 and said, 'I made really bad decisions.'

CHED EVANS

In April 2012, Sheffield United player Ched Evans was found guilty of rape and given a five-year jail sentence. He was released in October 2014 after serving half his sentence. When his appeal was rejected, he then applied to have his case reviewed by the Criminal Cases Review Commission. During the legal process, Evans' victim had to change her name and move house several times after harassment when her anonymity was breached.

Evans attempted to resurrect his football career, but potential deals with Sheffield United and Oldham saw public outcries, with an online petition receiving over 150,000 signatures. Fans were split between those wishing to give him another chance and others thinking it was not an appropriate signing for any club seeking to provide role models to youngsters.

Olympic pentathlon champion Jessica Ennis-Hill said she would ask for her name to be removed from an eponymously named stand at Sheffield United's ground Bramall Lane if Evans rejoined his former club. In April 2016 his conviction was quashed by appeal judges and a retrial was ordered. He was signed by Chesterfield in June 2016.

ADAM JOHNSON

In February 2016, Sunderland and England winger Adam Johnson admitted grooming and sexual activity with a 15-year-old girl. Johnson had communicated with the schoolgirl using social media and texts, exchanging over 800 messages, even when Johnson knew the girl's age. He met her in January 2016 and gave her a signed football jersey. His partner had given birth to their child a week after he began grooming the schoolgirl. They later separated. When the girl admitted to her parents what had taken place, the police were informed and Johnson was arrested. He was released from his contract by his club as the court case began. He was sentenced to six years in jail in March 2016.

CHEATING

Cheating can mean different things to different people. One person's innovative way of bending the rules is another's downright attempt to subvert the laws of the game. Here are some notable scandals where those involved were accused of not exactly playing fair.

KEY SCANDAL: LADDIE MARADONA

The 1986 football World Cup was held in Mexico. Argentina were blessed with the man in the number 10 jersey: Diego Maradona, one of the game's greatest players. His strength, ball control and ability to dictate games would be expressed in a tournament remembered mainly for his exploits.

Maradona had started his international career aged 16. He was too young for the 1978 World Cup and did not have a very successful time in Spain in 1982. But this was to be forgotten in the 1986 tournament. Maradona was captain of Argentina and he led them through the qualifying stages and past fellow South American team Uruguay in the first stage of the knockout games. In the quarter-final Argentina were to meet England, managed by Bobby Robson. England had struggled in the group games until reviving and beating Poland 3–0 with a Gary Lineker hat-trick. They repeated that scoreline against Paraguay in their first knockout game.

The Falklands War in 1982 between Britain and Argentina left over 900 people dead and it was inevitable that any sporting meeting between British and Argentinian teams would have extra layers of tension. The 1966 match in which Argentinian captain Antonio Rattin was sent off amid allegations of favouritism towards the English by the referee, and which saw the South Americans put out of the tournament, was also in many Argentinian minds.

The game was played on 22 June in Mexico City. At half-time the score was still 0–0 with England having survived Argentina's attacks. A few minutes into the second half, Argentina again attacked, with Maradona leading the charge. He played the ball forward to Jorge Valdano and continued his run, hoping for a return pass. England midfielder Steve Hodge attempted to clear the ball but missed it, sending it back towards his own net, the ball scooping up into the air. Maradona chased it and jumped. Then came the moment that forever defined him in the eyes of millions. As he jumped, England goalkeeper Peter Shilton came to punch the ball clear. He never got a touch, the ball going over his head, directed by a punch by the little number 10 in front of him. As the ball settled in the back of the net the Argentina players celebrated, while English players protested, unable to believe their eyes. But the goal stood.

Worse – or better depending on which flag you were flying that day – was to come only four minutes later. Maradona – who else? – was given the ball in his own half. He danced past three England players then began a run that took him all the way into the box, where he made Shilton commit before slipping the ball past him and into the net. It was voted in 2002 as the Goal of the Century. Few could disagree.

England scored with 10 minutes to go but could not get the equaliser. Argentina went on to beat Belgium in the semi-final, with Maradona scoring a great individual goal, before beating West Germany in the final.

Maradona said after the game with England, about his handball goal, that it was 'a little with the head of Maradona and a little with the hand of God'.

A FINE MESH

Being an ice hockey goaltender requires quick reflexes and strong nerves to face up to the puck when it's being directed at speed towards the goal area.

Tony Esposito was tending goal for the Chicago Blackhawks in 1969 when he devised a new way of preventing goals being scored through the 'five-hole' – the space between a goalie's legs.

A competitive player who did all he could to achieve shut-outs, he attached a piece of mesh netting across the space at the top of his legs. The addition to his normal equipment of mask, gloves and pads worked well until a rebounded puck almost hit an opposing player in the face. The governing body of the sport, the National Hockey League, brought in measures to prevent its future use.

BORIS DIS-ONISHCHENKO

Jim, I am very sorry.

Boris Onischenko to Jim Fox

The modern pentathlon at the 1976 Olympics in Montreal, Canada, consisted of:

- Showjumping

- Fencing

- Pistol shooting

- 200m freestyle swimming

- 3,000m cross-country running

After the first day's competition, the Soviet Union team were fourth, but their better events lay ahead. One of these was on the second day: the fencing. Among the Soviet pentathletes was Boris Onischenko, already a proven and successful competitor, who had won gold in the men's team event in 1972, going one better than the silver won at the 1968 games. He had also won silver in the individual event in 1972 and was expected to win gold in Montreal.

During his bout with Boris Onischenko, experienced British pentathlete Jim Fox became concerned that his opponent was scoring hits when his épée wasn't actually in contact. At one point he leaned back to avoid contact but a score was recorded. Fox duly protested.

An examination of Onischenko's épée showed it had a button installed that was able to activate the scoring circuit. Fox described it as a 'magic wand'.

The Russian and his teammates were disqualified and he was sent home in disgrace, eventually ending up becoming a taxi driver. The British team's performance suffered in the outrage, but they recovered and went on to win gold.

DISQUALIFIED QUALIFYING

Of all the sports, golf is the one that prides itself the most on its code of behaviour. Players have been known to call infringements on themselves, and those who bend or sail right over the rules face a lifetime of opprobrium and social banishment. From club golfers to the major professionals, you have to toe the line or you are in the rough.

Twenty-eight-year-old Scottish golfer David Robertson was playing in the qualifying rounds for the 1985 Open Championship when his caddie Paul Connolly was seen to walk off the course. Robertson was accused by his caddie of moving his ball – numerous times. Connolly said, 'On the ninth he got a free drop into thick rough. He asked me to go forward and check the yardage and when I got back, the ball was lying perfectly on a patch of grass.' One movement to get a better lie was by about 10 feet.

Robertson was disqualified on the fourteenth hole. It was his fourth misdemeanour. Other offences included handing in incorrect scorecards and marking his ball on the greens in the wrong place. He was fined £5,000 and banned for 20 years. The executive director for the European Tour, Ken Schofield, said: 'It's a sad day for golf.' Robertson had been a very good young player and had been Scottish boys' champion. He was later granted permission to play in amateur competitions.

VIJAY DAY

In the 1985 Indonesian Open, a young 22-year-old golfer called Vijay Singh faced missing the cut. When he finished his second round he was one shot over the cut-off limit of strokes. By the time he'd signed his card, he was no longer one shot over. He'd somehow lost a shot. He was banned from the Asian tour for two years as a result.

Singh went on to win three of golf's major tournaments but he was in trouble again in 2013 when he admitted using a spray that contained deer antler, which was said to help develop muscle mass and also aid recovery after injury. Unfortunately for him, it also contained IGF-1 (insulin-like growth factor-1), an anabolic muscle-growth hormone, which was on the World Anti-Doping Agency's banned substance list, and so Singh himself was banned by the Professional Golfers' Association (PGA) for 90 days. When he appealed, the case against him was dropped. Singh later sued the PGA for the way they'd handled the affair.

BACKHANDED

In rugby's 2002 Heineken Cup final, Leicester Tigers were playing Irish side Munster. Leicester were 15–9 up, with the game ticking down to its conclusion. Munster were awarded a scrum inside the English side's 22. As Munster's scrum half Peter Stringer prepared to put the ball into the scrum, Leicester's Neil Back, on the right-hand side of the scrum and close to Stringer, knocked the ball out of his hands and towards his own pack inside the scrum. The ball came out and Leicester cleared it. Moments later the whistle was blown and the game was over. Leicester had won.

Stringer complained to referee Joel Jutge, who was on the other side of the scrum at the time of the incident. He told Stringer he hadn't seen the incident, but Stringer's disgust was clear. He could be heard saying 'rubbish' to Jutge.

A comment on the BBC Sport's website following the incident read: 'As far as I'm concerned the Tigers will forever be known as the Cheetahs.'

PAM-ED OFF

American footballers are known for the amount of equipment they wear. They go to great lengths to be prepared for this high-contact game, using helmets, pads, gloves and so on. One thing that is not normally part of the gear is kitchen oil spray.

In November 2002, players from the Sacramento State Hornets college football team were spotted by a photographer applying PAM – a brand of non-stick cooking spray – onto their uniforms in a game against the Montana Grizzlies.

The ruse to make them harder to tackle didn't work. Sacramento lost 31–24. The Sacramento coach John Volek said, 'I have no knowledge of Sacramento State players using PAM.' Four players were reprimanded and Volek was sacked weeks later.

SAY IT AIN'T SOSA

6.06: A batter is out for illegal action when –
(d) He uses or attempts to use a bat that, in the umpire's judgment, has been altered or tampered with in such a way to improve the distance factor or cause an unusual reaction on the baseball. This includes, bats that are filled, flat-surfaced, nailed, hollowed, grooved or covered with a substance such as paraffin, wax, etc.

Major League Baseball Official Rules

Sammy Sosa from the Dominican Republic had a successful career playing for four Major League Baseball teams in America. He is the only player to have hit 60 home runs in a season three times and hit 609 home runs.

On 3 June 2003, Sosa was playing for the Chicago Cubs against Tampa Bay Devil Rays (now the Tampa Bay Rays). In the first innings he hit the ball and in doing so his bat broke into several pieces. The umpires immediately found it was a 'corked bat' – where the inside of the wooden bat is hollowed out and replaced with cork, to make it lighter and therefore easier to swing.

Sosa attempted to explain by saying it was a practice bat that had inadvertently been brought to the game. He was suspended for seven games.

MOVING THE GOALPOSTS

The phrase 'moving the goalposts' is a feature of the English language, being used to indicate a situation where the parameters are altered during a process or event. It's rarely used within football, as goalposts are immovable objects. Or at least they normally are. During a Swedish league match between IFK Gothenburg and Orebro in September 2009, the goalposts did move. Gothenburg's goalkeeper Kim Christensen was filmed lifting the posts and moving them in several inches, reducing the size of the goal. The referee spotted the infringement and moved them back. Christensen admitted he had done this several times before. Swedish football association official Khennet Tallinger said, 'I have never heard anything like this before. It's unique.'

HORRID HENRY

On 18 November 2009, Ireland played France in the Stade de France to claim a place in the 2010 football World Cup finals. In the first game of the two-match play-off, France had won 1–0. In the second game Ireland had scored to make it 1–1 on aggregate. Then, in the thirteenth minute of the first period of extra time, French striker Thierry Henry closed in on the goal as a long ball was directed into the box. Unable to control the ball with any legal means, the Barcelona player used his arm – twice – to help bring it down, whereupon he knocked it across the goal for William Gallas to score. Despite immediate and vehement protests, the goal stood. France went through. Henry admitted his foul play, saying: 'I will be honest, it was a handball. But I'm not the ref. I played it, the ref allowed it.'

Ireland continued their protests and demanded the game be replayed – something Henry himself agreed with – but it was to no avail and France went to South Africa for the finals, where they were eliminated in the first round. One Irish fan was so disgusted he said if France played England he would support England.

Ireland did not pursue their case against FIFA as an agreement was reached in January 2010 between the Football Association of Ireland (FAI) and FIFA. The agreement was attached to a confidentiality clause. A FIFA statement of 2015 explained: 'In January 2010 FIFA entered into an agreement with the FAI in order to put an end to any claims against FIFA. FIFA granted FAI a loan of $5 million for the construction of a stadium in Ireland.'

It seemed to many that the Irish had been bought off. The loan was to be paid back if Ireland qualified for the 2014 World Cup. As they didn't, it wasn't.

SALTMAN GETS HIS CHIPS

Scottish golfer Elliot Saltman was banned from the European Tour in 2011 for three months after being found guilty of not marking his ball correctly – five times in one round. Saltman was playing a tournament in Russia in September 2010 when his playing partners saw him repeatedly mark his ball in one spot and then replace it nearer to the hole.

CORRUPTION

Corruption occurs when the motives of a person in power are altered, usually by money but other factors can come into play, such as in the 1930s when Fascist Italy sought to use football for propaganda purposes. Iconic sporting events such as football World Cups and the Olympics have been tainted by corruption scandals, despite the best efforts of those involved to keep their activities secret.

KEY SCANDAL: FIFA

In May 2015, as they gathered for a meeting, senior FIFA officials were arrested by Swiss authorities. Some of the officials were arrested at the five-star luxury Baur au Lac hotel in Zurich. The arrests were the result of a three-year investigation by US authorities such as the FBI and the Internal Revenue Service, and saw 14 officials and corporate executives indicted on offences that included money laundering, racketeering and wire fraud. The US Department of Justice issued a statement that alleged the defendants participated in 'a 24-year scheme to enrich themselves through the corruption of international soccer'. FIFA officials were alleged to have taken bribes and kickbacks worth more than $150 million from US and South American sports marketing executives.

The nine officials who were indicted were:

Jeffrey Webb

FIFA vice president and Executive Committee member, CONCACAF president, Caribbean Football Union (CFU) Executive Committee member and Cayman Islands Football Association (CIFA) president.

Eduardo Li

FIFA Executive Committee member-elect, CONCACAF Executive Committee member and Costa Rican soccer federation (FEDEFUT) president.

Julio Rocha

FIFA development officer, former Central American Football Union (UNCAF) president and Nicaraguan football federation (FENIFUT) president.

Costas Takkas

Attaché to the CONCACAF president and former CIFA general secretary.

Jack Warner

Former FIFA vice president and Executive Committee member, CONCACAF president, CFU president and Trinidad and Tobago Football Federation (TTFF) special adviser.

Eugenio Figueredo

Current FIFA vice president and executive committee member, former CONMEBOL (South American Football Federation) president and Uruguayan football federation (AUF) president.

Rafael Esquivel
Current CONMEBOL Executive Committee member and Venezuelan football federation (FVF) president.

José Maria Marin
Current member of the FIFA organising committee for the Olympic football tournaments.

Nicolás Leoz
Former FIFA Executive Committee member and CONMEBOL president.

Other officials pleaded guilty:

Charles 'Chuck' Blazer
Former CONCACAF general secretary. Blazer had become an FBI informer in return for immunity from prosecution. He pled guilty to 10 charges of bribery, tax evasion and money laundering in November 2013.

Daryan Warner
Former FIFA development worker, son of Jack Warner, former CONCACAF president.

Qatar and Russia
As well as broadcast and marketing deals, the investigations looked at the bidding to host World Cups. In December 2010, football fans had been stunned when the winning bid to host the 2022 World Cup had come from Qatar. The tiny Middle Eastern state had no footballing history, had never qualified

for a World Cup and its location meant that in summer, when the games would be played, temperatures could reach 50°C. The decision to grant the prestigious tournament to Qatar, rather than Australia, Japan, the USA or Korea raised suspicions behind the bidding and voting process.

In March 2015, the tournament was moved back to November and December, to lessen the problems of playing and watching in the heat, but this caused controversy as it interfered with many countries' domestic schedule. The final was scheduled to be played a week before Christmas Day.

Eyebrows were also raised at the decision to grant Russia the 2018 World Cup. FIFA launched its own inquiry, headed by American lawyer Michael Garcia. When an executive summary of his report was released in November 2014, clearing the process of any claims of corruption, Garcia resigned. He said the summary contained 'numerous materially incomplete and erroneous representations of facts and conclusions'. Garcia said that he had found 'serious and wide-ranging issues' with the bidding and selection of the two host nations. The summary had been issued by Hans-Joachim Eckert, who was in charge of FIFA's adjudicatory chamber of the Ethics Committee.

Jack Warner

Much of the investigations centred on one of FIFA's six regional confederations: CONCACAF, which was headed by Jack Warner from 1990 to 2011. Warner had resigned in June 2011 following allegations that he was involved in vote-buying at a Caribbean Football Union meeting for the 2011 FIFA presidential election. Along with Warner, Mohammad Bin Hammam – who was standing for the presidency – was suspended by FIFA in May 2011. The 2011 election was subsequently won unopposed by Sepp Blatter, the long-reigning President of FIFA.

Warner was also implicated in illegal on-selling of tickets for the 2006 World Cup. When he resigned, a FIFA statement thanked him for his services to football and said: 'As a consequence of Mr Warner's self-determined resignation, all Ethics Committee procedures against him have been closed and the presumption of innocence is maintained.'

Sepp Blatter

On 21 December 2015, FIFA's Ethics Committee issued an eight-year ban for FIFA president Sepp Blatter. His banning was mainly due to him authorising a payment of 2 million Swiss francs (£1.35 million) to Michel Platini, the French former player and current president of UEFA and vice president of FIFA, in 2011.

In June 2015, only days after being elected president of FIFA for the fifth time, Blatter had said he would step down in February 2016. Platini had been mooted as a possible successor to Blatter; but as he was also banned in December 2015, this was now impossible.

Blatter had stated the payment to Platini was compensation for work the Frenchman had done previously, but the Ethics Committee found there was no basis for this payment to be made.

Jérôme Valcke

On 12 February 2016, Jérôme Valcke, former secretary general and right-hand man of Sepp Blatter, was barred from football for 12 years. The FIFA Ethics Committee stated he had been involved in misconduct over the selling of World Cup tickets. He was also fined 100,000 Swiss francs (£70,000).

New President

On 26 February 2016, FIFA members elected Italian Gianni Infantino as their new president. Infantino, who was general secretary of UEFA, said after his election, 'FIFA has gone through sad times, times of crisis. Those times are over.' In April 2016, Infantino was implicated in the Panama Papers scandal when documents leaked from legal firm Mossack Fonseca disclosed that in the period 2003 to 2006 he had co-signed contracts for the sale of TV rights of European football games to be shown in South America. The sale was to an Argentinian company called Cross Trading, who then sold the rights on for three times what they'd paid for them. Cross Trading was owned by an Argentinian called Hugo Jinkis, who was under investigation by US authorities for allegations of corruption over the sales of football media and marketing rights. Infantino, who was head of UEFA's legal services at the time, denied all involvement, saying: 'I am dismayed and will not accept that my integrity is being doubted.'

MUSSOLINI MEETS HIS MATCHES

Football's second-ever World Cup was held in Italy in 1934. The country's dictator Benito Mussolini, although not a football fan, could see the value for propaganda purposes, to show off his Fascist country in a good light. In order to do this he took control of many aspects of the tournament, including deciding on which referees would officiate matches.

In their first match, Italy beat the USA 7–1 and then met Spain. Italy were a rough team but faced little in the way of repercussions from the referee for any misdemeanours. The Spanish goalkeeper Ricardo Zamora, who was targeted for special treatment, was pushed over by one Italian, Angelo Schiavio, and then another, Giovanni Ferrari, put the ball over the line for Italy's only goal of the game. Belgian referee Louis Baert initially disallowed the goal, but after immediate pressure from the Italian players, allowed it to stand. The Spaniards had a goal disallowed for offside after their player, Ramón de la Fuente, had beaten four opponents before scoring. They managed to get one goal on the scoreboard and the 1–1 draw led to a replay.

The replay was played 24 hours after the first game, with seven Spanish players missing through injury, including goalkeeper Zamora. The Swiss referee René Marcet disallowed two Spanish goals – including one that was chalked off bizarrely to give a free kick to Spain – and Italy won 1–0. Their goal came after another contentious moment, with Spain protesting that their stand-in keeper Juan José Nogués had been obstructed before Giuseppe Meazza headed in.

In a sign that their performances left something to be desired, both referees from these two games were subsequently suspended on their return to their home countries.

In the semi-finals, Italy faced the tournament favourites, Austria, who were known as the 'Wunderteam' for their skilful and inventive play. In the nineteenth minute, a ball into the Austrian box saw Meazza bang into the Austrian keeper Platzer, the ball broke free and Enrique Guaita pushed it over the line. There were claims the goal was offside but it stood and Italy held on to their 1–0 lead to the game's end. At one point in the match the referee, Ivan Eklind from Sweden, headed the ball towards an Italian player; he had been wined and dined the night before the game by Mussolini.

In the final, Italy played Czechoslovakia. The referee chosen to officiate was Eklind again, who was invited to meet Mussolini before the game. Eklind was tolerant of the Italians' rough tactics, which included the talented Meazza punching an opponent in the stomach. It came as no surprise that Italy won and lifted the World Cup for the first time. Mussolini had achieved his goal.

BUNGED UP

George Graham was an Arsenal legend. As a player he was part of the team that won the League and FA Cup double in 1971. He became manager of the Highbury side in 1986 and led them to a thrilling league win in 1989, by beating Liverpool in the final minutes of the final match of the season. He won another league title in 1991, and other victories came in the League Cup (twice), FA Cup and European Cup Winners' Cup.

In July 1995, however, his reputation suffered as he was found guilty of having received illegal payments as part of a transfer deal. He received a total of £425,000 from a Norwegian agent, Rune Hauge, in December 1991 and August 1992 following the transfers of two players: Pal Lydersen who joined Arsenal in November 1991 and John Jensen who joined in 1992. Although Graham insisted it was an unsolicited gift, he was banned from football for a year. He returned the money.

Graham was sacked by Arsenal as a result of the scandal but returned to management following his suspension and took charge of Leeds United. He then joined Arsenal's arch-rivals Tottenham Hotspur in 1998 and with them won the League Cup in 1999.

In 2000, Graham said, 'I was wrong to accept the money. I concede that greed got the better of me. I should not have done it.'

UTAH NOT SAINTS

In June 1995, Salt Lake City in Utah, USA, was awarded the 2002 Winter Olympics. The city had bid four times before and the Salt Lake Olympic Organizing Committee (SLOC) had determined to secure the games for the city.

However, three years later, on 24 November 1998, a Utah TV station broadcast a report that one of the International Olympic Committee (IOC) members was having their child's university education paid for by SLOC. Sonia Essomba was the daughter of committee member Rene Essomba, of Cameroon. Hers was not an isolated example. It turned out that almost $400,000 was being paid in 'scholarships' to 13 individuals, six of whom were close family members of IOC members.

The IOC president, Juan Antonio Samaranch, ordered a review of these scholarships and other wider allegations. The commission was headed by Dick Pound. Other investigations were set up, by the US Olympic Committee, the FBI and by SLOC itself.

More claims appeared in the media about how money had been spent to bring the games to Utah:

- One IOC member's son had been given an internship by Salt Lake City's municipal organisation.

- Samaranch himself was reported to have received a present of guns from SLOC, but the president had not held on to them, donating them to the Olympic Museum.

- Jean-Claude Ganga, from the Congo, admitted to receiving $70,000 in cash.

- Ganga's mother-in-law had a knee replacement operation and his wife had plastic surgery paid for.

- Visiting IOC members were given free credit cards.

- Three members were treated to a visit to see the 1995 Super Bowl.

- Allegations surfaced that IOC members were supplied with prostitutes.

An IOC member called Marc Hodler claimed that bribery was common in securing votes for other cities bidding to host games, including Atlanta (Summer 1996) and Sydney (Summer 2000). Another Winter Olympic host had been Nagano, Japan, in 1998. There were reports that the bid committee had given, on average, $22,000 to the 62 IOC members who visited the bidding city. It wasn't possible to delve deeper into the bid committee's records as they didn't exist. All the records had been destroyed.

As a result of the scandal, ten IOC members lost their positions, either voluntarily through resignation or through expulsion. One other repercussion was that the process by which cities bid for hosting Olympic Games was amended to prevent such abuses in the future.

Tom Welch, who had been chief executive of SLOC's bid committee, and David Johnson, who had been vice president, were charged by the US Department of Justice with bribery and fraud offences but were acquitted in December 2003.

CHARLIE'S NOT MY DARLING

In July 2000, FIFA's Executive Committee members gathered together in Zurich to vote on choosing the host country for the 2006 football World Cup. The four candidates were England, Morocco, Germany and South Africa.

Morocco and England saw their bids eliminated in the initial rounds of voting, leaving the favourites South Africa, who had never hosted a World Cup, and Germany, who had last hosted the competition in 1974. If voting from the committee's 24 members resulted in a tie, FIFA president Sepp Blatter had said he would vote for South Africa.

In the final vote, South Africa was short by one vote. Germany had 12, South Africa 11. There was one vote missing. The vote belonged to 78-year-old Charlie Dempsey, the New Zealand president of the Oceania Federation. Dempsey had departed for New Zealand amid uproar, especially from the South African delegation, who were extremely upset to lose out. On his return home, Dempsey was met by the media, keen to find out why he had not voted.

It was widely believed that Dempsey had been instructed by his federation to vote for South Africa, once their first choice of England had been eliminated, but he denied this, saying he had been told to use his discretion. He stated that he didn't think his vote would matter as he expected the four Asian votes to be cast for South Africa. In the end, they went to Germany, persuaded at the last hour. Emmanuel Maradas, one of the South African bidding team, said: 'He had promised us that if England were eliminated before the final round, his vote would come to South Africa.'

Dempsey said he had been put under 'intolerable pressure' before the vote. He was bombarded with phone calls the night before the vote, including one from former South African president Nelson Mandela. He claimed to have been offered inducements to vote a certain way and also threatened that if he didn't vote for Germany, things might not be positive for Oceania nations in the future.

South Africa called for a revote but FIFA insisted the result would stand.

Dempsey resigned soon after the incident. He died in 2008. In 2015, investigative reporter Andrew Jennings alleged that a bribe was paid to him.

WADA STATE TO BE IN

On 3 December 2014, a German TV show called *Top Secret: How Russia Makes its Winners* alleged that Russian athletes had been doping and getting away with it due to the connivance of senior athletics officials at the International Association of Athletics Federations (IAAF). It claimed 225 athletes who displayed abnormal blood values weren't followed up properly by the athletics governing body.

One of the whistle-blowers was Liliya Shobukhova, the Russian marathon runner who won the London Marathon in 2010 and the Chicago Marathon three times from 2009 to 2011. She claimed that she was able to secure her place in the Russian Olympics team for London 2012 by paying officials €450,000 to ignore a 2011 positive doping test. Part of the money was later refunded when she was banned in 2014 after suspicious blood values were detected.

On 11 December, three senior figures at the IAAF resigned:

- Papa Masada Diack (IAAF marketing consultant, son of Lamine Diack, IAAF president)

- Valentin Balakhnichev (IAAF treasurer)

- Gabriel Dollé (IAAF anti-doping director)

Later that month the World Anti-Doping Agency (WADA) set up an independent commission to look into the allegations. Former WADA president Dick Pound was put in charge.

The fallout continued in 2015. In January, Valentin Maslakov, head coach of the Russian athletics team, resigned days after three Russian Olympic walking champions received suspensions for doping. The following month Valentin Balakhnichev resigned his position as president of the All-Russia Athletic Federation.

In April, the IAAF announced that the 2021 IAAF World Championships would be held in Eugene, Oregon, USA. This decision, without the normal bidding process, was lambasted by the head of rival bidding city Gothenburg. Bjorn Eriksson, the former head of the Swedish Athletics Association, said the decision showed 'an unacceptable lack of morals and transparency'. The decision was announced by Lamine Diack.

In August, German TV broadcaster ARD and *The Sunday Times* claimed that a third of the medals won at endurance events at the Olympics and World Championships from 2001 to 2012 – including the London Olympics – were given to athletes whose doping tests were suspicious. Later that month Lord Coe, the former Olympic champion athlete, became IAAF president, replacing Diack. In November, Diack, his adviser Habib Cisse and Gabriel Dollé were placed under investigation by French police.

In November, WADA published its first report: Russia was accused of state-sponsored doping and was provisionally suspended from international athletics by the IAAF. Russia declared it would work to improve its anti-doping practices.

Later that month Lord Coe resigned as an ambassador for sports company Nike. An email had emerged from a Nike executive suggesting that Lord Coe, the IAAF vice president, had lobbied Diack on behalf of Eugene. Nike had begun in Eugene and had strong links with the city. Coe claimed there was no conflict of interest but had resigned to stop the 'current noise level' surrounding the issue.

In December, there was more bad press for Coe as his aide, Nick Davies, resigned from his IAAF job when an email was released that showed him discussing Russian athletes who had been tested positive.

Papa Masata Diack, Valentin Balakhnichev and IAAF treasurer Alexei Melnikov were banned for life by the IAAF in January 2016. They were found to have been involved in blackmailing athletes and hiding positive doping tests. The findings stated: 'They acted dishonestly and corruptly and did unprecedented damage to the sport of track and field, which, by their actions, they have brought into serious disrepute.' Dollé, meanwhile, was banned for five years.

Later that month Lord Coe claimed there had been no cover-up. The next day WADA published its second report, stating that the IAAF council must have known of the doping issue. It stated: 'Lamine Diack was responsible for organising and enabling the conspiracy and corruption that took place in the IAAF.'

In July 2016, an attempt to overturn the ban on Russian track and field athletes from the Rio Olympics failed at the Court of Arbitration for Sport. Calls for all Russian competitors to be excluded from the Games came after the publication a few days previously of a WADA report which stated that Russia had administered state-sponsored doping, which took place in the 'vast majority' of sports from 2011 to 2015.

BAD DECISIONS

Many sports base their results on the decisions of third-party adjudicators in the form of referees, umpires, panels of judges and so on. Most of the time they carry out their duties responsibly, impartially and without controversy. But when they don't, scandal ensues.

KEY SCANDAL: BOXING NOT CLEVER

In boxing's light middleweight final at the 1988 Olympic Games in Seoul, America's Roy Jones faced South Korea's Park Si-hun. Boxing at the games had already seen controversy: South Korea's Byun Jong-il had seen decisions go against him from referee Keith Walker from New Zealand. Byun lost the bout as a result, whereupon his country's officials jumped into the ring to set about Walker. Byun then staged an hour-long protest by not moving from the ring.

Roy Jones had sailed through the competition while Park had not had such a straightforward journey. In the quarter-final against Italy's Vincenzo Nardiello his close victory resulted in Nardiello having to be dragged away from the officials, so angered was he by the decision.

Anyone thinking the judging at the final would be without incident was to be disappointed. Jones dominated the fight, landing 86 punches to Park's 32. The South Korean was given two standing eight counts and two warnings by the referee.

Before the decision, a US television commentator said, 'If he [Jones] doesn't win the gold off this I think then there's something rotten in Korea, because that was absolutely one of the most dominant things I've seen.'

Something was indeed rotten: Park was given the victory. When the decision was announced both boxers looked stunned. Heinz Birkle, a senior figure in AIBA (the world's international amateur boxing organisation), said: 'I want to hit them in the face. It's criminal.'

The judges were suspended and investigated but cleared of any wrongdoing. Rumours of bribery were not translated into evidence. Jones went on to become one of the top boxers of the 1990s. He had vowed never to wear his silver medal.

SKATEGATE

Ice skating is one of the most popular events of any Winter Olympics, but the spectators at the 2002 Winter Olympics in Salt Lake City were stunned when, at the pairs final, the gold was awarded to Russians Yelena Berezhnaya and Anton Sikharulidze instead of Canadian duo Jamie Salé and David Pelletier.

The Russians had made a technical mistake in their free skate, while the Canadians performed faultlessly. They had needed five 5.9 scores to win, but received four, from the USA, Canada, Germany and Japan; 5.8 marks were awarded by Russia, China, Poland, Ukraine and France. The Russians received seven 5.9s.

As the scores were announced, Salé and Pelletier sat stunned; Pelletier slumped with his head in his hands. Salé thought there had been a mistake that would be rectified. But it wasn't. The marks stood. She said later, 'I remember thinking, this is unfair.'

Immediately after the event, and also during the next day, French judge Marie-Reine Le Gougne admitted having pressure put on her to vote for the Russians. She later withdrew this claim.

The International Skating Union found that Le Gougne was guilty of collusion with Didier Gailhaguet, the president of the French Federation of Ice Sports. Both were banned from the sport for three years and from the 2006 Winter Olympics. Le Gougne and Gailhaguet were not pleased with their treatment. Gailhaguet said, 'This was an attempt to assassinate me politically,' and Le Gougne stated, 'I have been dragged through the mud. I have had my honour and dignity devalued. I have been attacked as a woman and been called the Bin Laden of figure skating.'

It was alleged that the Russians were given first place as part of a deal that saw reciprocal support for French skaters Marina Anissina and Gwendal Peizerat in the ice-dancing event. (The French pair won the event, although the Russian judge Alla Shekhovtsova did not vote for them.)

In an unprecedented move, Salé and Pelletier were awarded duplicate gold medals, while the Russian pair were allowed to keep theirs.

In August 2002, a Russian man called Alimzhan Tokhtakhounov was arrested in Italy in connection with charges relating to match-fixing the pairs and ice-dancing competitions at the 2002 games through bribery of officials. Tokhtakhounov, who is suspected of being a senior criminal gang figure in Russia, was released and he returned home. He is still wanted by Interpol.

THROWING IT OUT THE NET

Goalkeeper Roy Carroll signed for English football giants Manchester United in 2001 for £2.5 million. He was not first-choice keeper, having to compete with Fabian Barthez and then Tim Howard for his place between the sticks. In January 2005, Carroll was selected for a league game against Tottenham Hotspur, being played at Old Trafford. Instead of the number 1 jersey, he wore the number 13.

The game was nearing its end, with both teams not having scored. In the eighty-ninth minute, Spurs player Pedro Mendes hit a speculative long-range shot from the halfway line, hoping to lob it over Carroll, who was standing well off his line. Carroll ran back, covering the ball's descent, but when he attempted to catch it, he let it slip over him and into the net, the ball bouncing several feet behind the goal line. Not acknowledging this, he scooped it out and carried on playing. The referee and linesmen somehow missed the ball crossing the line and the game ended 0–0. Linesman Rob Lewis said afterwards, 'The Spurs player shot from distance and I was doing my primary job which was to stand in line with the last defender and watch for an offside. There was nothing I could have done differently apart from run faster than Linford Christie.'

Carroll's career was not blessed with barrel loads of good fortune. In the month after the 'no goal' goal, he was selected for the home game against AC Milan in the knockout stages of the Champions League. In the seventy-eighth minute Carroll failed to hold on to a long-range shot and Hernan Crespo scored the only goal of the game. Carroll was replaced by Tim Howard for the return leg, which was also lost 1–0 to the Italian club. Three months later Carroll was released by Manchester United.

He went on to play for a number of clubs but was unable to hold down a regular position. He played a trial for Sheffield United against Barnsley in March 2011 but let in two goals in under half an hour, and was sent off after giving away a penalty. A month later he entered the record books as the only manager to win a trophy on his only game in charge. He was temporarily put in charge of League Two side Barnet for the game against Stevenage in the Herts Senior Cup, which Barnet won 2–1.

Carroll's fortunes improved in 2012 when he signed with Greek side Olympiakos, where he became a fans' favourite after continuing to play while injured in a Europa League game. His first touch of the ball playing for them was to save a penalty. Carroll was later part of the Northern Ireland international team squad which qualified for the European Championships in 2016.

Interviewed in 2014, he said, 'If I was younger I'd be complaining, shouting, crying, but I have grown up and seen the wider world of football.'

MISCELLANEOUS

Some incidents defy easy categorisation. They inhabit their own unique place in the line-up of sporting scandals, be it a racehorse being kidnapped, a mysterious figure appearing mid-race on a ski slope, or international cricketers buzzing over a Test match in a biplane.

KEY SCANDAL: RUNNING POWER

America in 1968 was a turbulent place, with the ongoing Vietnam War, the assassinations of Robert Kennedy and Martin Luther King, and riots during the Democratic National Convention in Chicago. That year the Olympics were held in Mexico and the 200m men's final on 16 October was won by the USA's Tommie Smith. Second place was taken by Australia's Peter Norman and the bronze was won by America's John Carlos.

In the medal ceremony, both Americans walked to the podium without shoes and each wore a single black glove. When they stood for the national anthem, both men raised a gloved fist in a Black Power salute and bowed their heads. (As Carlos had forgotten his own gloves, each wore one of Smith's. The idea to do so was suggested by Norman, who also supported the protest by wearing a badge for the Olympic Project for Human Rights.)

There was an outcry over this political demonstration, with the IOC calling the silent protest 'a deliberate and violent breach of the fundamental principles of the Olympic spirit'. *Time* magazine called it a 'public display of petulance'.

The two Americans had also prepared other symbols: Smith's black scarf represented black pride, Carlos wore beads for black people who 'were lynched, or killed, that no one said a prayer for, that were hung and tarred. It was for those thrown off the side of the boats in the middle passage'. The not wearing of shoes represented black poverty.

Smith and Carlos were sent home from the games, with Smith noting afterwards, 'If I win I am an American, not a black American. But if I did something bad then they would say "a negro". We are black and we are proud of being black.'

HURRAY FOR THE WHITESHIRTS

The English team immediately made a good impression by raising their arms in the German salute while the band, after playing 'God Save the Queen', played the German national anthem.

The Times, 16 May 1938

In March 1938, the Anschluss saw Nazi Germany annexe neighbouring Austria. Hitler had reasoned that countries such as France and Britain would do nothing about it, and he was right. Britain was following a foreign policy known as appeasement, rather than confrontation.

Two months later, England were scheduled to play Germany in Berlin's Olympic Stadium. In the match played on 14 May, described as a 'splendid exhibition' by *The Times*, England, with star players such as Stanley Matthews, ran out 6–3 winners.

The result was not important, but the act of playing in Germany was seen by figures such as the British ambassador to Germany, Sir Neville Henderson, as a positive one in terms of international relations. Before the game England's players were advised by the Foreign Office to give the Nazi salute as a courtesy to their hosts and to foster good relations with the crowd. The Football Association agreed and pressure was put on those about to take part. The players were not 100 per cent behind the idea. One, Stan Cullis of Wolverhampton Wanderers, refused and was left out the team.

Giving the Nazi salute was unnecessary as Hitler wasn't at the game, although senior Nazi figures such as Rudolf Hess, Hermann Goering and Joseph Goebbels were. England captain Eddie Hapgood wrote later that giving the salute was 'the worst moment of my life'.

In 1935, Germany had played England at White Hart Lane, home of Tottenham Hotspur, a club with a large Jewish following. The match passed off peacefully, but the England players did not join in when the Germans extended their right arms in the notorious salute.

THE BIG FIGHT

Why should they ask me to put on a uniform and go ten thousand miles from home and drop bombs and bullets on brown people in Vietnam while so-called negro people in Louisville are treated like dogs and denied simple human rights?

Muhammad Ali, 1967

Muhammad Ali is one of sport's most renowned figures, whose fame goes well beyond the boxing ring. His boxing ability was allied with a sharp mind and a proud character that, while at times could be accused of showing arrogance, allowed him to stand up for what he believed in.

Born Cassius Clay in 1942, he fought his first professional fight in October 1960 when he beat Tunney Hunsaker. He was to face a bigger opponent seven years later when he took on the US government, by refusing to be drafted into the US armed forces during the Vietnam War.

Ali had changed his name from Cassius Clay following his conversion to Islam in 1964. He had grown up in Kentucky experiencing racial discrimination, and he allied himself with the Nation of Islam and its leaders Elijah Muhammad and Malcolm X, who advocated black rights. In April 1967, Ali had attended the draft in Houston, Texas, but refused to be inducted. Afterwards he issued a statement: 'I have searched my conscience and I find I cannot be true to my belief in my religion by accepting such a call.'

In 1964 Ali had originally been assessed for military service and categorised as being 1-Y, as his intelligence test was marked with such a low score. Using his trademark wit he commented on this, saying: 'I said I was the greatest, not the smartest.' By 1967, with the war in Vietnam escalating, his score was no longer seen as a barrier to service.

Ali lost his boxing licence immediately after his refused induction and this meant he did not fight for three and a half years. He was also stripped of the world heavyweight title he had held since 1964. He was prosecuted in the criminal justice system, convicted of evading the draft, fined $10,000 and given a five-year prison sentence, although he did not serve time behind bars due to his case going through the lengthy appeals procedure.

Ali began boxing again in 1970 once his licence had been restored, and in 1971 the Supreme Court overturned his criminal conviction. He regained his world heavyweight championship title in 1974 after beating George Foreman in the famous 'Rumble in the Jungle' fight in Zaire. Ali later lost his title but, aged 36, regained it for an unprecedented third time in 1978 in a fight against Leon Spinks. Acclaimed sports writer Hugh McIlvanney called it Ali's 'Third Coming'.

Ali finally retired from boxing in 1981 but was diagnosed with Parkinson's disease three years later. It has been thought that years of boxing and receiving countless blows to the head had been a contributing factor to the onset of his illness. He died in June 2016 after being admitted to hospital with respiratory problems.

ALL DOWNHILL

At the 1968 Winter Olympics in Grenoble, there were great expectations that Frenchman Jean-Claude Killy would be the local hero in the Alpine skiing events. He had won 12 out of 17 races in the World Cup circuit in 1967 and it was felt that he could win all three of the men's events. He started well: in the downhill, he won gold; and in the giant slalom, he also won gold.

In the slalom, Killy was fastest from the first run. In the second run, in foggy weather, he was slower and had to wait to see if anyone would beat his combined time. His closest rival was Karl Schranz of Austria, who had won silver in the giant slalom in the 1964 Winter Olympics. Schranz began his second run and then pulled up. He claimed a shadowy figure (described variously as a race official, another skier, a policeman or a soldier in differing accounts) had walked in front of him and affected his run, making him miss two gates. He was allowed to ski again, and his completed run beat Killy's time.

Killy's dream of an Olympic hat-trick was gone. Or at least until the race officials ruled that Schranz's missing of the gates was not caused by him encountering a mystery figure. He was disqualified.

Killy was the hero of the games, but Schranz was not happy. It was not just Schranz who had reason to be displeased. Another skier had also beaten Killy's time, but Norwegian Håkon Mjøen was also disqualified. The jury who decided the fate of the skiers was 50 per cent French. Had nationalist feelings overruled fair play? Schranz thought so: 'If Killy were sportsmanlike, he would refuse the gold medal.'

No matter the 'squalid bickering', as *The Times* newspaper described the controversy, the result stood and Killy's three golds made him the top medallist of the games.

TEQUENDAMA DRAMA

Bobby Moore was the captain of England who lifted the football World Cup on that sunny day in the summer of 1966. A ball-playing defender, he strode through matches, using expert timing to tackle opponents. Moore led his side to the 1970 World Cup finals in Mexico. They had a strong squad. Indeed, manager Sir Alf Ramsay thought it even stronger than the one that beat West Germany four years before.

To acclimatise for the tournament, England arranged to play two games in Colombia and Ecuador. Before the first game the England squad were staying in a hotel in Bogota, called Hotel Tequendama.

One evening after a team meal, Moore and Bobby Charlton went into a jeweller's shop called Fuego Verde ('Green Fire'), which was in the foyer of the hotel. They didn't see anything they fancied and didn't buy anything. As they left, the shop assistant accused them of stealing a diamond and emerald bracelet. They protested their innocence and were eventually released by security staff.

After their game in Ecuador, the team returned to Bogota and stayed at the same hotel. There was an unpleasant welcome for Moore, who was arrested. As his teammates departed for the imminent World Cup, their captain was detained for four days. He appeared in front of a judge who listened as the accusers said Moore dropped the bracelet into his blazer's left pocket. Moore was able to demonstrate there was no left pocket on his blazer.

The judge set Moore free. He rejoined his teammates and put the incident behind him, as he led England in their defence of the Jules Rimet trophy. In a group match against Brazil, Moore made one of football's great tackles when stopping the attacking Jairzinho just inside the box. England went out of the tournament at the quarter-final stage, being beaten 3–2 by West Germany. The tournament was won by Brazil, who defeated Italy 4–1 in the final.

COLT FORTY-FIVE

In any list of unsolved mysteries – not just those from the sporting world – the name of a famous champion racehorse remains a constant feature: Shergar. The colt had a glittering career, including winning the 1981 Epsom Derby by a record ten lengths, and by 1983 was retired from racing and kept as a prized stud. Shares in him sold for a total of £10 million and owners would pay £80,000 in stud fees to own a horse sired by the famous Shergar. It was kept at Ballymany Stud, located near The Curragh, the Republic of Ireland's main racecourse.

On the night of 8 February, a group of armed men in balaclavas appeared and took the horse away in a trailer. Shergar was never seen again.

There were delays in alerting the police, but three men were picked to be intermediaries with the kidnappers. One of them, David Thompson of ITV's racing team, spoke to a man on the telephone who eventually told him, 'The horse has had an accident. He's dead.'

What had happened? Various theories were expounded over the years but the most likely is that Shergar was kidnapped by the IRA, and when the kidnappers realised they were not going to get any ransom money, they shot the horse and buried his body in a bog.

FLIGHT INTO DANGER

You can either be heavy about it or you can treat it as a harmless prank.

David Gower

The Ashes series in Australia of 1990–1 saw England start badly. They had lost the first two Tests and drawn the third. In their non-Test matches they had lost to New South Wales before arriving at the Gold Coast's Carrara Oval near Brisbane to take on Queensland.

England players John Morris and David Gower were both out before lunch on the third day of the match. During lunch Gower suggested that as there was an airfield nearby and the players had seen civil planes flying over the ground, it might be nice to have a flight. Morris agreed. Being careful to check that England were still batting, they each climbed into a Tiger Moth biplane.

The aircraft were restricted to flying no lower than 2,000 feet in altitude, but Gower asked his pilot to go lower: 1,800 feet lower. His plane buzzed the ground, and England batsman Allan Lamb aimed his bat at Gower's plane as it flew overhead. Gower, who had thought it best not to alert his captain Graham Gooch to their plan, was soon in trouble as the press got wind of the flight.

Gower and Morris were hauled before a panel that included the England team's captain and manager Peter Lush and they were both fined £1,000. Lush called the stunt 'immature, ill-judged and ill-timed'.

The repercussions of the 20-minute flight did not end there. Gower's form deserted him for the rest of the tour and he only played another three Tests after the Ashes were over. Morris, who had hit a century before taking off, was never picked for England again.

POISONED

The Rugby Union World Cup final of 1995 was held at Ellis Park, Johannesburg, where host country South Africa met the All Blacks. President Nelson Mandela was in attendance at the final, his symbolic wearing of a South Africa jersey showing his desire for reconciliation in the once divided nation. The All Blacks were favourites to lift the Webb Ellis Cup, with Jonah Lomu in dynamic form. In the semi-final against England he scored four tries as his team notched a 45–29 victory.

In a close game, South Africa gained the vital advantage with a drop goal in extra time, the final score being 15–12. However, during the game some of the All Blacks were seen vomiting at the side of the pitch, and after the match was over it was revealed that 26 of the All Blacks' 37-strong party had suffered from food poisoning before the game. They had kept it quiet so as not to give the South Africans the advantage of knowing their opponents were in a weakened state.

The New Zealand coach, Laurie Mains, claimed that a waitress called Suzie had poisoned water given to the team and that the poisoning was a deliberate act to spoil the All Blacks' chances in the final. No evidence was found of a conspiracy and 'Suzie' was never located – but in 2000, Rory Steyn, the South African who was in charge of the security for the team, wrote in his autobiography, 'There is no doubt that the All Blacks were poisoned two days before the final.'

The team's manager, Colin Meads, thought the source of the illness might be milk that was off. The team's doctor, Mike Bowen, thought that urns containing tea and coffee had been tampered with. He said, 'It was unlikely to have been something that occurred incidentally or without some provocation, but I have no way of proving that was the case.'

As if the illness hadn't left a bad enough taste in the New Zealanders' mouths, there was more to come in the formal dinner to mark the end of the tournament. South African rugby president Louis Luyt made a speech in which he said, 'There were no true world champions in the 1987 and 1991 World Cups because South Africa were not there. We have proved our point.'

New Zealand had won the 1987 competition. The team got up and walked out, and the English and French parties joined them.

GAZZA TORN A STRIP

Celtic v Rangers games played in Glasgow are not just footballing encounters between city rivals but serve for many as a sectarian confrontation between Catholicism and Protestantism, and between Irish Republicans and Northern Irish Loyalists. In the 1980 Scottish Cup final, fans battled on the pitch at Hampden Park following a Celtic victory and the event led to a banning of alcohol within Scottish football grounds. These 'Old Firm' matches are always highly tense, highly charged games, and authorities are watchful to avoid any incidents that may incite crowd trouble. Players are warned beforehand accordingly.

In the New Year's game of January 1998, as England international Paul Gascoigne warmed up as a substitute for Rangers, he pretended to play the flute. To the innocent viewer this would generate a 'So what?' response. To anyone conversant with the symbols that lie behind the Old Firm game, this was a nod to Protestant flute bands. Gascoigne, no stranger to controversy, was fined £20,000 by his club, who sold him a few months later.

Gascoigne had also pretended to play the flute in 1995 after scoring in a pre-season friendly against Steaua Bucharesti. He'd protested innocence, claiming that other Rangers players had told him it was a normal way of celebrating a goal.

MATCH FIT

Brazil pride themselves on having star footballers that represent their country in playing attacking and attractive football. A list of the greats would have to contain Pelé, Garrincha, Rivelino, Jairzinho, Zico, Socrates and Ronaldinho. Another who would have to be included is Ronaldo, who first put on the famous yellow shirt in a game against Argentina in 1994. He was fast, possessed great dribbling skills and was able to pull off tricks to pass defenders on his way to goal. Although part of the winning World Cup squad of 1994, he didn't play in any of the games, yet by the next World Cup he was one of the world's best players, a key part of the Brazilian team.

In the final Brazil faced hosts France. When the team sheets were announced before the game there was one notable name missing: Ronaldo. Then with 40 minutes to kick-off his name reappeared. He came on to the pitch and started the game but the Ronaldo that had mesmerised the crowds, scoring four goals in the tournament, was missing and his team were beaten 3–0.

Speculation raged as to the reasons behind this massive shock. Was he injured? Had he a secret medical condition that had been unearthed? Had he been drugged by rivals France? Had he been drugged by his own team, who'd given him a sleeping pill by mistake?

It transpired that in the afternoon before the final Ronaldo had suffered a convulsive fit, in which he lapsed into unconsciousness for 3–4 minutes. He was taken to hospital but tests found nothing untoward. After leaving hospital he went to the stadium and insisted he was fit to play. Rumours spread that Brazil's sponsors Nike had applied pressure to ensure that he played but these were denied. The Brazilian team had signed a lucrative sponsorship deal with Nike two years before. The team doctor Lidio Toledo later said, 'Imagine if I stopped him playing and Brazil lost. At that moment I'd have to go and live on the North Pole.'

In 2002 a Brazilian newspaper alleged that Ronaldo's fit was caused by an injection of xylocaine, an anaesthetic that if not correctly injected can cause a fit. In 2014 the striker himself said, 'Was it pressure or nerves? It could be.'

THE ITALIAN RAPSCALLION

Italian striker Paolo Di Canio was not the shy, retiring sort of footballer who slipped quietly through his career. He entered the British game when he signed for Celtic in 1996. Before this he had played in Italy for Lazio, Juventus, Napoli and AC Milan. He became a firm favourite of the fans with his exciting and inventive playing style but left the Glasgow club after one season, following a dispute with owner Fergus McCann over money.

He signed for Sheffield Wednesday and it was here he ran into trouble during a match with Arsenal in September 1998. The game, which was won by Wednesday 1–0, boiled over when Di Canio and Martin Keown squared off against each other in the middle of a fracas after Arsenal's Patrick

Vieira and Wednesday's Petter Rudi had tussled. Keown and Di Canio were shown the red card and the Italian reacted by pushing referee Paul Alcock, who staggered backwards before falling dramatically. Di Canio was fined £10,000 and banned for 11 games. He left the club for West Ham, feeling that Wednesday could have done more to defend him.

Showing his individualism, he won a FIFA Fair Play award in 2001 after stopping play by catching the ball when the Everton goalkeeper Paul Gerrard was lying injured. The game was 1–1 and Di Canio was in the penalty box and had a clear opportunity to score.

He returned to Italy in 2004 and joined Lazio. More controversy came when he gave a Fascist salute during the derby against Roma in 2005. He received a thank-you letter from Alessandra Mussolini, granddaughter of Italy's former Fascist dictator.

In 2013, Di Canio was appointed manager of Sunderland, amid controversy due to his political beliefs. He lasted six months before being sacked. He had said in 2006, 'Yes, I'm a Fascist, so what? I'm not racist.'

NOT LAND OF MY FATHERS

Shane Howarth was a full-back and Brett Sinkinson a flanker for the Welsh national rugby union side. Howarth won 19 caps and Sinkinson 20. Both were born in New Zealand but claimed the right to play for Wales through their grandparents.

There was one slight problem with their international appearances: they had no legitimate reason to play for Wales. In 2000, a scandal broke following an investigation by the

Glasgow Herald that looked at their official birth records in New Zealand.

Sinkinson's grandfather on his father's side wasn't from Wales, as believed, but from Oldham in England, where he worked as a slaughterman. Sinkinson's agent defended his player's claim, saying that Oldham wasn't very far from Wales. (Oldham is 190 miles from the Welsh town of Carmarthen that had been claimed as the grandfather's place of origin.) Sinkinson was quoted as saying, 'I don't know a thing about my Welsh grandfather. When I came over here, it was mainly to bum around and see the sights.'

For Howarth, although he claimed his mother's father was from Cardiff, the birth records stated that his mother was a Maori. He then claimed his Maori grandmother had a child with an unnamed Welshman, although this wasn't backed up by the records.

The players were barred from playing any more games but Sinkinson later played for Wales under residency rules. Howarth was unable to play as new rules that were brought in meant his four caps for the All Blacks ruled him out.

The Welsh Rugby Union (WRU) were criticised for allowing non-Welsh players to play without adequately checking their credentials. Former Welsh captain Jonathan Davies said, 'It makes my blood boil to think we've left out fully qualified, proud Welsh boys in order to allow a couple of foreigners to indulge their own fantasies. What an utter disgrace.'

They weren't the only players whose legitimacy to play internationally was in question. Prop Dave Hilton played for Scotland 41 times before he was embroiled in the affair that was termed 'Grannygate'. It was found that his 'Scottish' grandfather hailed from Bristol and not Edinburgh as he and his own father had thought. Hilton was later able to play one more time for Scotland due to residency criteria. In his final game he helped Scotland beat South Africa.

THE ROAD TO VANDERLEI

It is hard enough to win an Olympics marathon medal when things run smoothly, but it shows great powers of fortitude to win one after being attacked mid-race by a protestor. In the 2004 marathon at the Athens Olympics, Brazilian Vanderlei de Lima was leading with 4 miles to go when an Irishman dressed in a short kilt ran across his path and grabbed him, forcing him into the side of the road and into the crowd. A following policeman dismounted from his bicycle and joined spectators as they tried to both free the runner and apprehend the race intruder.

De Lima got free and was able to return to the race but he was overtaken by the eventual race winner, Italy's Stefano Baldini, and Mebrahtom Keflezighi of the USA. The intruder, a former priest, had performed a similar stunt on the track at the British Grand Prix the previous year.

De Lima said after the race, 'If it were not for that lunatic, I am sure I would have won the gold. He did not injure me, but he broke my rhythm and I lost concentration.' As well as his bronze, de Lima was awarded the Pierre de Coubertin Medal. The medal, named after the founder of the Olympic Games, is awarded for those who symbolise the spirit of the games. Less than 20 have been awarded since their inauguration in 1964.

The Brazilian athletics authority appealed to the IOC to have de Lima awarded a duplicate gold but the race results were made to stand and no second gold was awarded.

A year after the marathon, Brazilian beach volleyball player Emanuel Rego offered his own gold medal from the 2004 Olympics to de Lima, but the runner said, 'I'm happy with mine. It's bronze but it means gold.'

SPYGATE

Formula One is a sport in which success is reliant on constant technological development. Improvements in a team's racing cars come through innovations in design put into practice by their in-house engineers. To help the drive for improvement, teams are always keen to be aware of any changes in their opponents' cars, looking for measures that could be applied to their own machines.

One way of finding out what your competitors are doing is to be in possession of technical documents they have produced, and this is what happened in 2007 when McLaren were found to have information on Ferrari's 2008 car.

Ferrari were alerted when a worker in a photocopying shop in England noticed that a woman had brought in almost 800 pages bearing the Ferrari logo to be copied onto disc. His suspicions led him to contact the Italian manufacturer. The woman who had come into the shop turned out to be the wife of Mike Coughlan, chief designer of the McLaren team.

Investigations found that the source of the leaked documents was Ferrari's head of development, Nigel Stepney, who had become unhappy with recent changes at the Italian team. Stepney was a friend of Coughlan, both having worked for the Lotus team in the 1980s.

Stepney was sacked and later given a 20-month custodial sentence by an Italian court for industrial espionage, which he did not serve. He was killed in a road accident in 2014.

Coughlan had been suspended by McLaren, who initially denied that any other member of the team had any knowledge of the leaked information. The World Motor Sport Council (WMSC) ruled there was no evidence to prove McLaren had acted on the information from Ferrari. However, more details came to light when emails between McLaren's drivers were produced showing that McLaren were aware of the information. In September 2007, the WMSC fined the team $100 million and disqualified them from the 2007 Constructors' Championship. This was the biggest fine in sporting history. Coughlan was banned from F1 for two years.

In November 2007, the FIA announced that Renault were also to be investigated for possession of data from another team, this time McLaren. In December 2007, the WMSC found the team guilty but did not issue any disciplinary sanctions.

KEYS TO THE DOOR

Scotsman Andy Gray was a combative striker, who played for clubs such as Dundee United, Aston Villa, Wolves, Everton and Rangers. After he finished his playing career in 1990, he became a TV football pundit for Sky Sports.

In 2011, off-air comments that he and presenter Richard Keys had made about female assistant referee Sian Massey, before a game between Wolves and Liverpool in January

2011, were leaked. In their conversation they questioned the ability of women to understand the offside rule.

When more evidence of sexist behaviour was revealed, including that towards a female colleague at Sky, whom Gray had asked to place a microphone in his trousers, Gray was sacked. Richard Keys soon followed out the door after resigning when footage emerged of him asking ex-footballer Jamie Redknapp if he had had sex with a particular woman, using the phrase 'Did you smash it?'.

Gray and Keys were employed by talkSPORT before joining Qatari broadcaster beIN Sports. Five years after their ignominious departure, Keys tweeted Andy Gray, celebrating the anniversary of 'one of the biggest carve-ups in TV history'.

DOUBLE FAULTS

Each March the BNP Paribas Open is held at Indian Wells in California. It forms part of the schedule for the men's Association of Tennis Professionals (ATP) and the Women's Tennis Association (WTA).

The 2016 event was overshadowed by comments made before the women's final by the tournament's chief executive Raymond Moore. He was quoted talking derogatively about women's tennis, saying: 'If I was a lady player, I'd go down every night on my knees and thank god that Roger Federer and Rafa Nadal were born because they have carried this sport. They really have.' He claimed the women's tour rode on the coat-tails of the men's tour and remarked on the attractive qualities of some of the female players.

Moore apologised but the furore did not abate and he resigned soon after. He wasn't the only one to spark controversy at the event. The winner of the men's tournament, Novak Djokovic, said that male players should get more prize money as they attracted more spectators. He said, 'Women should fight for what they think they deserve and we should fight for what we think we deserve.'

GREEN AND WHYTE BLUES

The biggest organised cheating scandal in the history of Scottish football – probably British football and possibly in British sport.

Alex Thomson, Channel 4, November 2015

Rangers FC were formed in Glasgow in 1872. The club's Ibrox stadium was built in Govan, on the south side of the city, near to the shipyards where many of the club's supporters worked. Rangers and city rivals Celtic (formed in 1887) formed the 'Old Firm', with both teams vying for supremacy, while also realising the rivalry was good for business – both clubs have the biggest number of supporters in Scottish football, with Celtic having a larger stadium than the national team's at Hampden Park. In 1971, 66 Rangers fans were killed following a crush on a stairwell and as a result the stadium was redesigned, ushering in a modern football ground that became all seated and was able to accommodate over 50,000 people.

Rangers had not had a majority owner throughout its history until in 1985, when the John Lawrence Group, under the chairmanship of Lawrence Marlborough, gained 52 per cent of the shares. In 1988 these shares were sold to

Scottish businessman David Murray for £6 million. Under Marlborough, Rangers had appointed Scotland and Liverpool midfielder Graeme Souness as player-manager and had brought in top England stars such as goalkeeper Chris Woods and captain Terry Butcher. This was a foretaste of things to come as Murray embarked on an ambitious project to develop Rangers as a force in European football. High-profile players continued to be brought to Ibrox, including England star Paul Gascoigne, Dutchman Ronald de Boer and Danish winger Brian Laudrup.

In 1997, Rangers equalled Celtic's feat of winning nine league titles in a row, but an historic tenth championship was denied the following summer by the Parkhead side. Success in Europe was not as forthcoming as domestically, although Rangers reached the last four of the European Champions League in 1993, losing out to Marseille for a place in the final.

Murray had encapsulated the feeling of the times by saying in 1998, 'For every five pounds Celtic spend, we will spend ten,' and spend the club did. In 2000, Rangers signed Norwegian striker Tore Andre Flo for £12 million from Chelsea, but such spending had a cost – in the 2003–4 season, Rangers' net debt reached £73.9 million. Murray took measures to reduce the debt, which included a share issue in 2004 that raised £51 million, which he underwrote. In 2006 a deal with retail company JJB Sports also brought in much-needed money. Murray announced he wished to sell his shares in the club in July 2006 and did so in 2011 when Craig Whyte bought them for £1. Murray's companies had suffered following the economic downturn that began in 2008 and he was unable to offer financial assistance to the club as before.

There was another legacy that was to cause severe problems for Rangers. From 2001 until 2010 the club had used Employee Benefit Trusts (EBTs), which allowed the club to offer tax-free loans to its top players rather than pay them directly. They were abolished by the government in 2011.

In 2010, in what was known as the 'Big Tax Case', HMRC pursued Rangers for £35 million of tax and £14 million in penalties, due from the EBTs.

Rangers contested it through a first-tier tribunal and in November 2012 the tribunal ruled in favour of Rangers. This decision was upheld in 2014, but the Court of Session ruled in November 2015 that tax and National Insurance should have been paid. Lord Drummond Young said when delivering the verdict, 'The law is clear: the payments made in respect of footballers were in our view derived from their employment and thus the payments were emoluments or earnings.'

In May 2011, Craig Whyte had said, 'As a keen Rangers supporter, I now look forward to helping the club secure its future as a leading force in Scottish and European football,' but events were to be somewhat different. Under Whyte, Rangers went into administration in February 2012. The administrators, Duff & Phelps, listed 276 creditors, who were owed £55 million. The club had not paid any PAYE tax or VAT and faced a £9 million bill, as well as the potential tens of millions from the Big Tax Case. As a result, Rangers were deducted 10 points, and subsequently finished 20 points behind league winners Celtic.

In June 2012, HMRC refused to accept a proposed company voluntary arrangement as it would not return sufficient money to the club's creditors. The club was to be liquidated.

Soon after, Rangers' 'business and assets' were sold for £5.5 million to a company called Sevco Scotland Ltd, owned by a consortium headed by Charles Green, which was later renamed 'The Rangers Football Club Ltd'. In April 2012, the administrators Duff & Phelps had valued the club's assets as being over £125 million. Rangers were formally liquidated on 31 October 2012.

In the summer of 2012, there was much discussion as to whether Rangers the football club still existed or whether they were a newly formed entity. At the start of the 2012–13 season the 'newco' Rangers, who had their application to play in the top division rejected, began playing in the Scottish Third Division. Their first match was at Glebe Park, against Brechin City in the Ramsden Cup in July.

The Scottish Premier League began an investigation under Lord Nimmo Smith which in February 2013 fined the 'old' Rangers £250,000 for its use of 'side-letter' arrangements in which its players were paid 'very substantial payments' through offshore EBTs, which were not disclosed to the football authorities. Nimmo Smith did not find Rangers had gained any sporting advantage.

The going was not smooth for the new owners and Green left his position as chief executive in April 2013 and then resigned from his position as a paid consultant to the club in August that year. The huge focus on the club aroused strong feelings. BBC journalist Jim Spence was threatened in September 2013 after talking on radio about 'the old club that died'.

In October 2015, charges of fraud were made against several of the men involved in the acquisition of the club. All charges except those against Craig Whyte were subsequently dropped.

The ownership and running of the club, which had been the focus of much attention for several years, saw another chapter being written in May 2015 when South African-based businessman Dave King was appointed chairman.

In April 2016, having been promoted successively from lower divisions, Rangers won the Scottish Championship title (formerly the First Division) and so secured a place in the Scottish Premiership for the 2016–17 season.

CONCLUSION

The history of sporting scandals is long and there seems no reason to suggest it will end any time soon. The human desire to win at any cost – or lose for a beneficial price – is one that is unlikely to disappear. With expanding global audiences providing increased revenues for sport, it may even grow.

Innovative ways to cheat will continue to be found, in order to gain that vital edge in performance. In early 2016, for example, the world governing body for cycling confirmed that they had uncovered the first ever case of 'technological doping' when a cyclo-cross bike ridden by Belgian rider Femke van den Driessche was found to have an electro-magnetic motor installed under the seat. She was subsequently banned for six years.

And innovation might be tied to other developments in human activity. As has been shown, incidents of bad behaviour have occurred across a wide spectrum of sports, and perhaps new sports as yet unplayed will also see their participants conniving in how to subvert the rules.

One thing that is certain is our interest – and perhaps a certain delighted outrage – will not diminish in watching as our sporting icons continue to misbehave.

SOURCES

Newspapers and Magazines

Adelaide Advertiser
Autosport
Belfast Telegraph
The Celtic View
Cycling News
Daily Mail
Daily Mirror
Daily Record
Daily Telegraph
Glasgow Herald
Golf Digest
Golf Week
The Guardian
Herald Sun
The Independent
Irish Examiner
Irish Independent
The Irish Times
Los Angeles Times
New York Daily News
The New York Times
The New Yorker
The New Zealand Herald

Rolling Stone
Ski
Skiing
Smithsonian
Sports Illustrated
Sunday Mail
Sunday Mirror
The Scotsman
The Sun
The Times
USA Today
The Washington Post

Books

Ball, Phil *Morbo: The Story of Spanish Football* (When Saturday Comes, 2001)

Bonner, Packie *The Last Line: My Autobiography* (Random House, 2015)

Dawson, Jeff *Back Home: England and the 1970 World Cup* (Orion, 2012)

Ferdinand, Rio *Rio* (Hachette, 2014)

Fotheringham, William *Racing Hard: 20 Tumultuous Years in Cycling* (Faber and Faber, 2013)

Gordon, Richard *Scotland '74: A World Cup Story* (Black & White, 2014)

Halliday, Stephen *Amazing and Extraordinary Facts: Olympics* (David & Charles, 2012)

Hay, Davie *The Quiet Assassin: The Davie Hay Story* (Black & White, 2009)

SOURCES

Huggins, Mike 'Lord Bentinck, the Jockey Club and Racing Morality in Mid-Nineteenth Century England: The "Running Rein" Derby Revisited', *The International Journal of the History of Sport* (December 1996)

Jennings, Andrew *The Dirty Game: Uncovering the Scandal at FIFA* (Century, 2015)

Kohn, George C. *The New Encyclopedia of American Scandal* (Infobase Publishing, 2001)

Kynaston, David *WG's Birthday Party* (Bloomsbury, 2011)

Mac Giolla Bhain, Phil *Downfall: How Rangers FC Self-Destructed* (Frontline Noir, 2012)

Moore, Richard *The Dirtiest Race in History: Ben Johnson, Carl Lewis and the 1988 Olympic 100m Final* (A&C Black, 2013)

Nelson, Murry R. *American Sports: A History of Icons, Idols, and Ideas* (ABC-CLIO, 2013)

O'Reilly, Emma *The Race to Truth: Blowing the Whistle on Lance Armstrong and Cycling's Doping Culture* (Bantam Press, 2014)

Orejan, Jaime *Football/Soccer: History and Tactics* (McFarland, 2011)

Owen, Paul *The Joy of Running: For Those Who Love to Run* (Summersdale, 2013)

Pattullo, Alan *In Search of Duncan Ferguson* (Mainstream, 2011)

Perry, John *Rogues, Rotters, Rascals and Cheats: The Greatest Sporting Scandals* (John Blake, 2007)

Radford, Brian *Caught Out: Shocking Revelations of Corruption in International Cricket* (John Blake, 2012)

Rae, Simon *W. G. Grace: A Life* (Faber & Faber, 1998)

Rice, Jonathan (Editor) *Wisden on Grace: An Anthology* (Bloomsbury, 2015)

Rippon, Anton *Amazing and Extraordinary Facts: Football* (David & Charles, 2012)

Robinson, Neil *Long Shot Summer: The Year of Four England Cricket Captains 1988* (Amberley Publishing, 2015)

Rowbottom, Mike *Foul Play: The Dark Arts of Cheating in Sport* (Bloomsbury, 2013)

Sanders, Richard *Beastly Fury* (Random House, 2010)

Sharpe, Graham *Free the Manchester United One: The Inside Story of Football's Greatest Scam* (Pavilion, 2014)

Slade, Michael J. *The History of the English Football League: Part One 1888–1930* (Strategic Book Publishing, 2013)

Spurling, Jon *Death or Glory! The Dark History of the World Cup* (VSP, 2010)

Ward, Andrew *Football's Strangest Matches: Extraordinary but True Stories from Over a Century of Football* (Pavilion Books, 2013)

Wisden Cricketers' Almanack 2003 (John Wisden & Co, 2003)

Woodland, Les *The Yellow Jersey Companion to the Tour de France* (Random House, 2007)

Websites

AllOutCricket   www.alloutcricket.com

Associated Press   www.ap.org

BBC   www.bbc.co.uk

Bleacher Report   www.bleacherreport.com/uk

BMW Berlin Marathon   www.bmw-berlin-marathon.com

British Athletics   www.britishathletics.org.uk

Cricket Country   www.cricketcountry.com

SOURCES

Deadspin   deadspin.com
ESPN   www.espn.co.uk
ESPN Cricinfo   www.espncricinfo.com
ESPN Scrum   www.espn.co.uk/rugby
Formula One   www.formula1.com
FourFourTwo   www.fourfourtwo.com
Fox News   www.foxnews.com
Futbol de Primera   www.futbolprimera.es
GrandPrix.com   www.grandprix.com
History   www.history.com
International Paralympic Committee   www.paralympic.org
ITV   www.itv.com
Journal of Olympic History   isoh.org
Judiciary of Scotland   www.scotland-judiciary.org.uk
LFCHistory.net   www.lfchistory.net
Liverpool FC   www.liverpoolfc.com
Major League Baseball   mlb.mlb.comhome
Manchester United   www.manutd.com
Olympic Games   www.olympic.org
Ouest-France   www.ouest-france.fr
ProPublica   www.propublica.org
Reuters   uk.reuters.com
SBNation   www.sbnation.com
Scottish Rugby Union   www.scottishrugby.org
Sky Sports   www.skysports.com
Slate Magazine   www.slate.com
SoccerBase   www.soccerbase.com
South African History Online   www.sahistory.org.za
Sports Reference   www.sports-reference.com
The Smoking Gun   www.thesmokinggun.com

The State Hornet   www.statehornet.com
The Sweet Science   www.thesweetscience.com
UEFA   www.uefa.com
Wisden India   www.wisdenindia.com
WorldSoccer.com   www.worldsoccer.com

TV and Radio

Fascism and Football (TV documentary, BBC, 2003)
Tennis: Game, Set and Fix? (File on 4, BBC Radio 4, January
    2016)

Other

*European Rugby Cup Decision of Appeal Committee in Appeal
    by Tom Williams* (European Professional Club Rugby, 2009)

ACKNOWLEDGEMENTS

Thanks go to those fine people at Summersdale who make the task of creating a book that much easier through their professionalism, support and attention to detail.

Special thanks go to Claire Plimmer for firing the starting pistol and Robert Drew and Emily Kearns for their patient and thorough work in getting the project over the finishing line without having to flash too many yellow cards.

Thanks also to Hamish Braid for his work up front in designing the cover and to Carol Turner who swept up the errors in the proofreading midfield.

At the end of the day the vast majority of sportsmen and women entertain and inspire without a whiff of scandal and this book is dedicated to them.

THE WORLD'S TOUGHEST RACES

FROM THE MOST EXTREME TO THE DOWNRIGHT WEIRD

ALI CLARKE

THE WORLD'S TOUGHEST RACES

FROM THE MOST EXTREME TO THE DOWNRIGHT WEIRD

ALI CLARKE

ISBN: 978 1 953 730 8   Paperback   £8.99

What do *fierljeppen*, running 156 miles in the Sahara Desert and coal-carrying all have in common? They're just some of the wackiest, toughest and most extreme manpower races and challenges ever dreamt up.

This fact-packed miscellany is bursting with all the details, statistics and anecdotes of the world's most unusual competitions (ever heard of bog snorkelling?) and intense endurance contests (how does the Death Race sound?).

Whether you're an armchair thrill-seeker or you're wild enough to have an adventure or two under your belt, this book will entertain and inspire.

The
BUMPER
B⬤OK
of
SPORTING
WIT

Richard Benson

THE BUMPER BOOK OF SPORTING WIT

RICHARD BENSON

ISBN: 978 1 953 917 3   Paperback   £9.99

When I lost my decathlon
world record I took it like a man.
I only cried for ten hours.

Daley Thompson

Win, lose or draw, players and fans always have something
to say about it. Packed to the rafters with the best quips
and quotes from across the world of sport, this massive
collection will keep you smiling in the stands even when
you're smarting from the scoreline.

Have you enjoyed this book?
If so, why not write a review on your favourite website?

If you're interested in finding out more about our books,
find us on Facebook at **Summersdale Publishers** and
follow us on Twitter at **@Summersdale**.

Thanks very much for buying this Summersdale book.

www.summersdale.com